"*Mom . . . and Loving It!* is not only a breath of fresh air but [also] a lifeline for exhausted or discouraged mothers today. With vulnerability and reality, [Sharon and Laurie] offer hope and help for the challenges moms face today."

—Cheri Fuller,
Speaker and Bestselling Author of *When Mothers Pray*

"When you read this book you'll be convinced Sharon and Laurie were eavesdropping in your house. They cover the nitty gritty of motherhood with pointed, powerful practicality. . . ."

—Kathy Collard Miller,
Speaker and Author of *Partly Cloudy with Scattered Worries*

"Mom, you really don't want to miss reading this book. You will be inspired and renewed in knowing that mothering is truly a wonderful divine calling. . . ."

—Fern Nichols,
Founder and President, Moms in Touch International

"This life-giving book is filled with personal stories, vision, encouragement, and biblical training that shows how to walk with God through the many issues of motherhood."

—Sally Clarkson,
Author, Speaker, Director of Whole Heart Ministries

mom...
and
loving it!

sharon lovejoy autry

laurie lovejoy hilliard

BETHANYHOUSE

MINNEAPOLIS, MINNESOTA

Mom . . . and Loving It!
Copyright © 2005
Sharon Lovejoy Autry and Laurie Lovejoy Hilliard

Cover design by Diane Whisner

Published by Bethany House Publishers
11400 Hampshire Avenue South
Bloomington, Minnesota 55438

Bethany House Publishers is a division of
Baker Publishing Group, Grand Rapids, Michigan.

Printed in the United States of America

Library of Congress Cataloging-in-Publication Data

Autry, Sharon Lovejoy.
    Mom—and loving it! : finding contentment in real life / by Sharon Lovejoy Autry and Laurie Lovejoy Hilliard.
       p. cm.
    Summary: "Two sisters with six children between them help other moms set aside unrealistic expectations to find fresh purpose and contentment in nurturing their families. Discussion questions with each chapter make this book ideal for groups as well as individuals"—Provided by publisher.
    ISBN 0-7642-0039-9 (pbk.)
    1. Motherhood—Religious aspects—Christianity. 2. Mothers—Religious life.
I. Hilliard, Laurie Lovejoy. II. Title.
    BV4529.18.A88   2005
    248.8'431—dc22   2004024662

dedication

To our Mom,
who reminded us at each stage of our lives
that she loved every minute.
You were and are a great example
of a "mom ... and loving it."
We love you.

Acknowledgments

to our sweet husbands who have sacrificed *much* to lead in the ministry God has called our families to. Thank you for filling in the gaps when we had to be gone for long hours of writing and for encouraging us through the slumps. We are so blessed to call you ours!

to our children, Alec, Abby, Avery, Brittlea, Crislynn, and Davis, for being you! Your notes, treasures, and hugs kept us going. We are so proud of all of you and absolutely love being your moms. We love you oodles and bunches!

to our dad and mom, Hank and Rita Lovejoy, for giving us a love for families. Thanks for always believing in us and being excited about what God is doing in our lives!

to Chris and Lesa Lovejoy, our brother and sister-in-law, for your encouragement to step out and stand on what God called us to do! Kalie and Courtney, what sweet spirits God has given you. You're precious to us!

to Dinina, our sanity! Your help at just the right times is priceless. We are glad to call you not just our kid-sitter but also our friend!

to Nonie and AnnNan for reading and summarizing books for us, and to D-Daddy for believing in us. We love you!

to Grrdaddy and Nohnie for your support and encouragement, and free baby-sitting!

to GeneAnn, Barry, Brett, and Bri: Thank you for your encouragement along the way.

to Jeanne, our sweet editor, for having patience and confidence in us as "first-time" writers. Your calm voice was reassuring.

to Kyle and Suzanne Duncan at Bethany House, for being sensitive to God's prompting on our behalf.

to Janet for being excited with us and for walking us gracefully through the book publishing process.

to Joe and Dee Dee Clark for the writing haven you provided for us ... (and the chocolate right when we needed it!)

to Uncle Jack and Aunt Myna for allowing us to have a piece of paradise at your cabin in Colorado while writing last summer.

to Janie Henry for being a regular Bible concordance as well as a wonderful prayer partner!

to Stacia for helping me (Laurie) get through chapter 14, which we dedicate to "baby Hannah."

to all the moms across the country who provided a wealth of insight and information through their personal stories. Thanks for being vulnerable!

to our Lord and Savior, our hope. We realize that we are only here by your grace and it is for your glory that this book was written.

contents

introduction

Mom . . . and Loving It! It sounds so noble, but if you are anything like us, you struggle at times to find real enjoyment in this thing called "motherhood." Adding children to your life may have sounded so glamorous and fulfilling, but you and I quickly realized it was the most challenging job we'd ever taken on. Many times all the demands and expectations of motherhood leave us with feelings of guilt and inadequacy, asking ourselves, "Why am I not enjoying this time in my life?" Or, "Can I do this?" We live with secret struggles that we don't dare share with anyone because we feel so bad about them. Our guilt often grows into bitterness and resentment because we can't live up to the ideal mom that lives in our minds. Contentment seems like a lofty, unattainable goal—way out there.

So how *do* we find contentment in the real lives we live as mothers? *Mom . . . and Loving It!* is a *real* book. It is not a book that lays out cliché answers to hard questions. It is a book that contains *real* stories from *real* moms with *real* struggles and *real* victories. As you read through the pages of this book we hope you will be comforted to find that you are not alone. To be a mom and loving it is a process that takes time. Thankfully, God is able to change our perspective—from feelings of simply surviving motherhood to actually enjoying it.

Whether you are a mom, a stepmom, a single mom, or a mom of special-needs kids, this book is for you. You will find hope and encouragement rather than condemnation as you read through these pages. You will be renewed to work at the job of motherhood with wholehearted devotion!

This avenue of communication is new to us, and we are excited and humbled to have the opportunity to share with you. We have already met many of you as we have traveled across the country as 2MOMS (with 2 dads and 6 wonderful children), speaking to many of your moms groups. You are the inspiration for our writing *Mom . . . and Loving It!*

How to use this book
(Group or Individual Study)

Mom . . . and Loving It! is great for group or individual study. However, if possible, we encourage you to find another mom (or group of moms) to work through the book with you. The time you spend together each week will not only reinforce what you've read but also build friendships that could last a lifetime. Perhaps there is a mom across the street that you've wanted to get to know. This would be a great way to build a relationship with her. A neighborhood group study would work well since it would offer convenience as well as an opportunity to meet after the kids go to bed.

When reading the book as a group study, we suggest that you read two chapters a week for seven weeks. Then the final week, you'll have only one chapter to discuss. At the end of each chapter you'll find a section entitled *Stop, Drop, and Restore Your Soul* followed by *Making the Most of the Moments*.

Stop, Drop, and Restore Your Soul

In this section there are discussion questions designed to encourage you to stop, drop what you're doing, and search your soul. They will be thought-provoking and great conversation-starters. Whether you are going through the book by yourself or with a group, you will probably want to have a journal to record your answers to the questions at the end of each chapter.

This section also includes a pre-written prayer. Feel free to use the prayers we have included at the end of each chapter to help you compose your own prayers. You might even begin your time of reading with prayer, asking God to open your heart to hear and understand what He wants you to learn.

Making the Most of the Moments

In this section you'll find practical ideas to help you apply what has been discussed in each chapter. If you're going through the book as a group, share with one another which ideas you implemented and how they were helpful. Just because there may be as many as five ideas in this section, don't feel like you have to fit all of them into your week. They are just suggestions.

Use this book as it best fits into your life

We know you are busy moms and we are humbled that you have picked up our book and are taking the time to read it! We know your time is very valuable. If you need to skip a page, skip a page. If you are a single mom and want to skip the chapters on marriage, just jump over those and keep going. If your time is really limited, look through the table of contents and find the chapter that you most need to read at this moment in time. Skipping around is okay.

In Appendix 1 you'll find a list of resources that can give you additional help in a variety of areas (they are categorized by topic) and the names of organizations that minister specifically to moms.

Enjoy yourself, have fun, and be encouraged; God knew what He was doing when He called *you* to be a *mom*. Even if you are not a mom who is loving it right now, we pray that God will grow you into one by the time you've finished this book.

We'd love to pray with you before you begin . . .

Father,

Thank You for this precious mom who is holding this book in her hands. We pray that You will make Your love known to her as she reads through the pages ahead. Give her hope, Lord, that You will provide the strength she needs to love and enjoy this challenging, exhausting, and rewarding job of "motherhood." Help her find contentment in the real life she is living. Give her peace—not as the world gives—but the kind of peace that can only be found in You. Remind her, Father, that hands-on mothering won't last forever. Help her to find ways to enjoy the special moments she has today.

We know You are going to accomplish great things in the life of this dear mom. And when Your will is accomplished, we will give You all the glory and praise! In Jesus' name we pray. Amen.

chapter **one**

i'm going to love being a mom!

When the Ideal Meets Reality

No one prepared me for the sacrifice of being the mommy!
Charlotte

Don't brashly announce what you're going to do tomorrow;
you don't know the first thing about tomorrow.
(PROVERBS 27:1 THE MESSAGE)

my husband and I (Laurie) tied the knot when we were twenty-three years old. We decided we wanted time together before kids, so we intentionally waited five years before starting a family. I just knew (but would never have told anyone) that because we were "more mature," we would be the best parents ever! We both had great examples from our parents, and, on top of that, we had degrees in social work; we were sure that would make us much better parents. I worked full-time during pregnancy and felt great. Things were busy . . . but all was going according to the plan.

I was going to "get" to be a "stay-at-home" mom, and, boy, was I ready for a break from my crazy routine. I was sure that after the baby came I would have more time to cook healthy meals, keep the house clean (no more dusty baseboards!), and exercise. I would finally have time to do some things I had been waiting to do. So during the busy months prior to my baby's arrival, I began making a long list of "to do's" for the time when I would be home with the baby. I was sure I would have more time *then*. I was anticipating the arrival of our new little one—sure that things were going to work out just as planned!

But ten days before my twenty-ninth birthday, and five weeks before my due date, I began having contractions. My doctor instructed me to go home, drink lots of water, and lie down. My husband decided this would be the perfect time for me to watch the Lamaze videos he had checked out from the library (since we hadn't made time to go to the classes). As I was watching the video and practicing my breathing techniques I felt a gush of water. This was not part of my plan! My husband was panicking as I shouted orders at him. He made phone calls to our families, then drove me (over the bumpiest road ever) to the hospital. This wasn't what I had expected!

Thoughts began rushing through my head: "Lord, please help my baby be all right; I'm scared! I'm not supposed to be having this baby yet—it's not time. I don't have his room finished . . . his bed isn't even painted. I don't think I'm ready. I don't know how to breathe right through these contractions, and they are already hurting!"

Fourteen hours later Alec Andrew Hilliard was born in Dallas, Texas, at Baylor Hospital. For a preemie, he was a healthy six-pound boy. After staying in the hospital only one extra day, we took our bundle of joy home. In our shock and amazement we felt thankful (and relieved) that it was all over.

Now maybe we could get back to the "plan." Things were going to calm down. I was sure life was going to be wonderful, just like my baby boy.

It wasn't long before I realized that everything wasn't wonderful. I was not in control of *the plan* anymore. Postpartum blues set in like a cloud of gloom every afternoon. Sitting outside (waiting for my husband to come home, angry if he was two minutes late), I would see ladies driving home, listening to songs all by themselves. I envied them.

I was getting very little sleep and was having trouble coping with life. My husband tried to help by taking us on drives, just to get us out of the house. My thoughts and emotions were going crazy: "I hadn't *planned* on feeling like this . . . I have everything to be thankful for . . . a healthy baby, wonderful husband, and supportive family. What is wrong with me?" I really thought motherhood would be different, easier, more enjoyable. I always thought there would be an immediate bond between my baby and me, but I didn't feel I knew him very well. At times I didn't even know if I *liked* him. (It's hard to like a baby who cries all the time.) "What if I can't do this?"

My life felt far from "normal," and the sleepless nights and exhausting days were taking their toll. Alec cried much of the night and some of the day too. I wasn't getting anything done around the house and couldn't understand why. I would tell myself, "Surely this little 'blob' of a baby couldn't be robbing me of so much time and sanity. I'm supposed to have *more* time, not less!" There were days I would find myself still in my nightgown at four in the afternoon, and I hadn't even *thought* about supper yet. "So much for healthy meals," I thought. My husband was lucky if I found time to make macaroni and cheese. I would look around at my mess of a house and think, "I know I've been busy all day, but there is no evidence to prove it!"

The whole "mommy" role was much harder and more demanding than I expected. My "to do" list was getting longer instead of shorter. Time with my husband and friends was almost nonexistent. I longed for some kind of balance in my life. I hadn't been out with any of my girl friends in months and I really needed a break. Even though I was finally getting more sleep and my emotions were not as crazy, I was still struggling to figure out how to adjust to my new role as "mother" and still be the same "me" as before. I thought to myself, "I'm sure things are going to get easier and I'm going to be content with motherhood. Maybe *later,* when he can do more for himself my plan will work. *Later,* when I have a little more of *my* life back, I'll be content."

To Be Continued . . . (in chapter 15)

B.C. (before children) expectations

Like Laurie, before I (Sharon) was a mom I had whimsical, unrealistic dreams of what life as a mother would be. "The best is yet to come," I thought. If there was a "Best Mom" award, I just knew I would walk away with the trophy. I would be the best of them all! Even though I saw other women struggling in their role as a mother, I could always see the "obvious solution." I determined that I would be great.

Were you like me, with a superhuman view of the mom you would be? My guess is that you might have had some of these same B.C. thoughts that I did:

- I will enjoy every minute! I will keep a record of my kids' lives through journals and scrapbooks, **and**
- I will scrapbook for **all** of my children, not just the first one.
- I will not allow my children to throw a fit in public.
- I will have a clean house, clean baby, clean clothes . . . all the time. I'm choosing to stay home, for heaven's sake! What else will I do with my time? (Oh, brother!)
- Even though I'm not very patient with other children, I'll be better with my own. (I guess I thought there was some kind of hormonal happy pill or something.)
- When we eat out I will be in control of my children, teaching them to sit quietly.
- I will have my figure back at my six-week checkup.
- I'll teach my child not to grab the candy at the checkout counter. (Now, how did I think I was going to do that?)
- Other people might have trouble with their teens, but I just know we'll have a close relationship.
- I won't yell at my children. If we do have difficult moments, I'll use those times as teachable moments. (Oh, whatever!)

What know-it-all inexperience! If you're a mom, you have to be smiling by now, not just because of those crazy, overblown ideas, but because before you had children, some of the same thoughts crossed your mind too. The expectations we have for ourselves and our children can cloud our view of reality until we literally can't see straight! Elisa Morgan and Carol Kuykendall in *Real Moms* say:

> "B.C. (Before Children), most of us formed in our minds certain pictures of perfect mom-dom, which still linger today. . . . No wonder one mom wistfully remarked, 'I was a better mom before I had children.'"[1]

With all the cute clothes and sweet smells of babies we somehow missed the realities of extra expense, loads and loads of laundry, daily meals to prepare, books to read, appointments to keep, exhaustion from lack of sleep, and the loss of free time. Before kids, my husband and I would spontaneously go on dates any day of the week. One of our favorite pastimes was hanging out in bookstores, looking through travel magazines and children's books. I'm glad I bought kids' books then because I don't have the budget or the time to peruse the kids' section anymore. How times change!

everything was black and white

Don't you remember seeing parents with their children and shaking your head at their lack of intervention when the child was screaming, pouting, or generally acting out? A mom (Cindi) shared, "I would watch my friends with children and I would just know how I would have dealt with such-and-such a situation—and of course, my way would have worked! When I actually had my own children it was a shock to discover that I had absolutely no idea how to parent this life that was now my responsibility." Before children every problem, every conflict, every misbehavior had a black-and-white solution.

Before I had children this was my black-and-white theory: If children throw a fit, you don't allow it. If they argue, you don't allow it. Maybe they don't clean up their mess—you don't allow that either. The problem was, I never went through the process of figuring out the "don't allow it" part. How do you do that? (See Appendix one for resources.) Since becoming a mom my black-and-white theories have turned into many shades of gray!

B.C. I never thought about having to deal with the same struggles over and over, even though as a first-year schoolteacher I was told by some more-experienced teachers to go over the rules not just the first day but every day, for weeks. They advised me that kids forget and need to be reminded. The same is true in our homes as we train our own children. Just because I correct my children's manners one time doesn't mean they will remember the next time they sit down at the table. And what do you do with their fears? When they are scared at bedtime and you get them to sleep one night, that doesn't mean they won't have the same fear the next night. When they feel inadequate in some area, like reading, athletics, or music, you can't simply "take care of the problem" and move on. It's a process, with each day adding to the process.

When there is a breakthrough, and the end of one stage is in sight, I've learned not to get cocky about how great we are as parents. Usually there is another stage coming, and it could arrive any minute! My hus-band always says, "There are no easy solutions." He's right—especially in parenting. Just because we correct the behavior, calm the fear, or encour-age them through a trial, it doesn't necessarily mean it will disappear for good. As parents we are thankful for the little victories along the way, knowing that there will be another challenge around the corner. That's normal.

getting to know you

Before I had children I would look at moms struggling with a defiant child and wonder why they weren't correcting the kid. I never stopped to consider the depth of knowledge and understanding that they had about their children. It was easy for me to be judgmental toward these mothers when I had no clue what it was like to be a mom. I was think-ing that a stern word or a firm squeeze would have been appropriate, but these parents knew how their child would respond. I had heard that every child was different, but surely that didn't mean you needed differ-ent ways to discipline them. After all, that wouldn't be fair, would it?

Just like everybody said, children *are* different. For example, in our family all of our children are capable of being selfish at times but they deal with it in different ways. One child has a hard time realizing she is wrong and takes some extra nudging to apologize, while with the other all it takes is a stern look and she is ready to ask for forgiveness. Learning to deal with those differences is a lifelong process. Like building with Legos, each experience with our children adds a new block of informa-tion to the structure of our relationship with them. We have the chance to let each new challenge that arises in our parenting push us closer to God as we ask Him for His help.

> "The number of decisions you make regarding your children is enormous. If you are sure you are doing what is right, you will sel-dom ask the hard questions and be open to the answers God wants to offer. . . . These questions compel you to ask and seek God's answers to your parenting problems, thus keeping your heart open to new levels of trust in God."[2]

God has gifted us as moms to know our children, but it doesn't just happen when they enter your home. It takes work. More than anyone else (at least until they are married), we can know what makes our children tick. They are complex, active, happy, pouty, selfish, full-of-life beings, and it takes time to get to know who they are and how they work.

expectations change

When our first child was only a couple of months old, my husband and I (Sharon) decided we could still carry on our day-after-Christmas shopping spree, even with our infant. As I walked through the store, I happened to be by myself, but was following a mom with a crying child. The flustered mom passed a girl in her late teens who commented to a friend, "I can't believe anybody would bring a baby out on the day after Christmas!" I silently laughed because I was one of those crazy people out with a baby, but also because I remembered thinking the same thing! Then I smiled as I thought about the teenager, "Just wait . . . you'll believe it one day! You'll try to do it all too."

What are moms supposed to do? Give up all the things we think are fun, now that we have children? Surely not, but we do live and learn. Some things are too hard to be worth the pleasure, but that's okay because there are other pleasures that we didn't have before children joined our lives. For the moment, we no longer have an annual shopping spree after Christmas. We're too busy resting up from the long Santa night we just had. But one day, we'll hit the stores again!

stop, drop, and restore your soul

How many of your pre-motherhood expectations did you carry with you into motherhood? Unfortunately, most of us don't drop our expectations once the children arrive. Instead, we add reality to our ideals, leaving us trying to attain unreachable goals. Did you read that? Unreachable! Trying to live up to unreachable goals leaves us feeling discontent and produces unbearable guilt (which will be addressed in the following chapter).

1. What were your ideals before you had children? How did your "plan" change after you had them?
2. What advice would you give a first-time mom-to-be?
3. What unreachable goals do you need to let go of? (Here are

some examples: shopping with coupons, keeping up with friends, scrapbooking, making homemade bread, always having a craft ready, etc.)

4. What do you think God really wants from you as a mom?

5. What stage is your child going through right now? How has God used your children and their challenging phases to mature you as a person?

Lord,

We thank You for the privilege of being moms. Though we are at different stages in this journey, our similarities are overwhelming. We have made (or will make) countless meals for them, we will drive miles and miles to see them, stay up when they are sick or out late to make sure they are all right, kiss away hundreds of hurts, wish we could kiss away other hurts, cry tears of heartache and tears of joy, discipline, say yes, say no, all because we long for our children to be respectful adults. We love our children more than life, Lord, even when they make ridiculous choices. As our children grow and change, continue to grow and change us into the moms we need to be—the moms You know we can be: Moms who love being moms. We trust You and know that You really didn't make a mistake when You allowed us to enter this exhausting, time-consuming, mind-boggling, but joy-filled world of mothering. Just as we hold a frightened child during a storm, hold us tight, Lord, through every stage of motherhood.

We pray this in Jesus' name ... Amen.

making the most of the moments

1. **memories** When you have time today, look through some of your photos, even if they're in a shoe box. (They are easier to put on the fridge if they're not in a scrapbook!) Put out some pictures of your children when they were babies or some that you haven't seen in a while and leave them up for a few days.

2. **what's in a letter?** Write your child a letter, sharing specific ways you have grown as a person since he or she became a part of your life. Even if they aren't able to read it on their own, you can read it to them. Save your letter to give to them when they are older.

3. **growing mom** Ask God during the day, "As my children grow and change, Lord, please grow me as a mom." You might even pick up a potted flower while you're out, to put in your kitchen window. When you see it, let it be a reminder to pray for your children as they grow, and for yourself as you grow too. Blessings!

chapter two

why do i feel so guilty?

Three Guilt Grenades Common to Moms

---

*My mom told me that you really don't understand the word
GUILT until you have children ... she was right.*
Chantelle

My guilt has overwhelmed me like a burden too heavy to bear.

(PSALM 38:4)

S he realized I was a mom too, and with little prompting, she began to
pour out her heart like a rushing waterfall. "I told my husband for
years, 'I was meant to be a mom.' But when I finally became a mom I
found myself yelling, too busy to stop and play. I knew I was missing the
moment but I didn't know how to stop. I would think, 'My time with
my daughter is going to be gone soon!' Sometimes at night, when she is
sleeping peacefully, I go into her room, sit by her bed, and cry, asking
God to forgive me for yelling at her. I feel so *guilty*. Why can't I do this?"
With tenderness in her eyes for her daughter, but tears of disappointment
with her failure as a mom, she looked at me longingly, hoping to hear
that she wasn't alone in her struggle.

Was she the failure she thought herself to be? If she is, then so am I,
and so is every mom who has ever lived. This disheartened mom shared
the thoughts and summed up the feelings of all of us at one time or
another. Why the guilt? We thought we would be better than we are.
Our B.C. expectations somehow found their way into our "after children" lives. We expected that we would be perfect. Many times we still
hold on to expectations for ourselves that are too high, producing guilt
beyond measure. Another mom shared her story:

All my life I wanted to be a wife and mother. God had other

plans for a while as I finished college, became a teacher, and still wasn't married. And then God chose to bless me above my wildest expectations and allowed me to marry one of my best friends, whom I had admired for years! And then my son arrived, the first of the children I had always dreamed of having. And, wow, reality check! All that sleep-deprivation, and nursing him all the time. I felt like no one had truly prepared me for the sacrifice of being the mommy!

Being a mom, every day, every hour, every minute is like adding a whole new world to your life.

"Before kids, my perspective was all about me and all about my marriage; i.e., who I was in relation to my husband. It was so much easier to figure out who I was when my biggest tangible input came from only one other person. Now there are four children thrown in, all with different personalities" (Suzanne).

Before we had children, our time—mine and yours—was dedicated to ourselves and our husbands. Our eyes were free to see his needs and our own needs. The files of our minds weren't cluttered with feeding schedules, sorting out-grown clothes . . . again, or getting fidgety kids to finish their homework. We did the things we *needed* to do—working, spending time with hubby, building friendships—and still had plenty of time to do the things we *wanted* to do—shop, talk on the phone, sleep late. With most of our time now spoken for, it's no wonder we moms often find ourselves discontented, questioning this consuming, self-sacrificing role. When the idea of how things "should be" clashes with reality, guilt begins to fall on a mom's shoulders. The result: fatigue, lack of patience, feelings of failure and hopelessness, and wondering if we really were "meant to be moms."

the guilt experts

Moms are experts at many things, like hearing a crying child in the night, managing naps and extracurricular activities, juggling Twinkies and juice boxes, cooking, cleaning, and running a taxi service. But one area we moms particularly excel in is our ability to dwell on our inadequacies, failures, and flops. When it comes to guilt, moms are the experts! A couple of moms shared with us their thoughts on guilt: "We try to do so much and when our expectations aren't met we feel we have failed" (Kelly). "My guilt surfaces when I expect too much of myself and I once again fail—I fail myself, my family, everyone it seems! Yet often my expectations are unrealistic" (MaryAnn).

Here are just a few of the things we "guilt experts" expect of ourselves and feel guilty about when they don't happen:

- I don't feed my kids enough vegetables.

- I shouldn't be so moody—happy, then sad. How can my family keep up with my roller-coaster state of mind?

- I don't spend as much time with my children as Jane does. . . . She is a great mom!

- The car is such a mess. Why can't we keep it clean?

- I let my kids talk me into anything. I'm too easy. I wish I could stick with my "no."

- You mean it was my week to bring snacks? I can't seem to remember anything lately!

- I don't think I've read to my kids in a week. They're going to get behind in school, and it will be my fault!

- My daughter makes me furious. She always thinks she has a better way of doing things. The thing is, she *does* have good ideas. Why can't I think more like a mom? I feel so incompetent!

- I'm harder on my children in front of my parents (or in-laws) because I know they think I'm too lenient as a mom.

- Sometimes I just don't like him. How can I not like my own son? I must be a terrible mom!

- I don't know why God ever allowed me to have children. I was pretty good when they were little, but now that they're older, I'm lost. I don't know how to do this! It's so much harder than I thought it would be. We can't seem to communicate about anything.

- I'm so tired. When I'm exhausted I have a hard time making our home a fun place to be.

- I know I should have taken them to the dentist by now, but I just haven't been able to get it all together.

- She's driving me crazy! I had a right to yell and set her down force-fully, didn't I?

- I accused her unjustly and immediately I knew I was wrong. Why can't I just listen before I answer or accuse?

- I tell him, "Why don't you act your age?" Then I realize he is!

- We had to borrow a baseball glove! How in the world could we come to a baseball game and not remember the glove? I even for-got my lawn chair.

With that kind of stress, it's no wonder we sometimes miss the joy in our role as mothers. Should these expectations and desires be so important to us? They only lead to frustration, disappointment, worry, and regret—summed up, we have a weight called guilt tied around our necks that we carry around as though we're required to wear it. In a survey, we asked moms what caused them the most guilt. There were three distinct areas that rose to the top of the responses: lack of time with their families, whether to work in the home or away, and anger issues. We'll talk about these more in-depth in the next three chapters, but here's a summary of what moms shared with us.

guilt grenade #1: lack of family time

The interesting thing about this topic is that these concerns came from moms who work outside the home as well as stay-at-home moms. Both feel guilty for not spending enough time with their families.

- I feel the most guilt from having to do mundane chores like laundry, grocery shopping, etc. when my kids just want to play or have my undivided attention. I also feel guilt when their normal kid stuff irritates me. (Sarah—California)

- Having a sense of not spending enough time with my husband and our children is the source of most guilt in my life. (Ann—Mississippi)

- The thing that probably causes the most guilt for me is when I give in to the temptation to let other things crowd my time so that I don't have time to be the wife and mother that I should and want to be. (Charlotte—Indiana)

- I feel the most guilt from not spending enough time playing with my children. (Patti—California)

- I have guilt regarding the quality time I spend with my children. It seems like I'm always dragging them here and there and not making enough time to just play. (Jessica—Georgia)

- I think it is very challenging in this time we live in to find a balance between the work/home environments. I do work out of my home and feel that my "paid job" never goes away. I always seem preoccupied with deadlines and feel tremendous guilt not being able to separate work and home. (Stephanie—Texas)

guilt grenade #2: stay-at-home and go-to-work guilt

Moms who work outside the home feel guilty for being away, missing events, or being preoccupied with all that has to be done. But moms who stay at home sometimes feel guilty too—for not helping out financially or for "wasting" their talents and abilities. Here are comments from some of these "guilty" moms:

- Working outside the home and being away from my child during the day produces the most guilt in my life. (Devonna—Texas)

- Most of my guilt is due to the stress of needing to work full-time and therefore not being able to attend every field trip or every school function my children have. Although I try to work my vacation schedules around these events, there are usually one or two that I cannot attend and it kills me! Also, [I feel guilty for] having to use "after care" and not being able to pick up my child from school each day. (Pamela—Colorado)

- The most guilt in my life [comes from] knowing that there are so many things my husband wants for us financially and I want to help him. But we don't want to trade our children being home with me by putting them in day care. (Heather—Texas)

- I sometimes feel guilty that I'm not doing enough to help out financially. (Diane—Minnesota)

guilt grenade #3: dealing with angry outbursts

All moms become angry at one time or another, but when we get angry at our children, we feel like we are alone in our failures. These comments from moms across the country let us know that we aren't alone in our struggle with angry outbursts.

- I struggle with guilt a lot because I feel like I mess up a lot. There is an extreme amount of pressure [I] put upon myself, to be the best mom I can be, and sometimes I mess up and do things I wish I hadn't, like yell at my kids. (Michelle—Minnesota)

- The thing that produces the most guilt in my life is my anger. I allow myself to be angered by pettiness, which hurts my relationship with my children. I am not the calm, controlled, patient mom that I want so desperately to be when I allow anger to get a foothold. (Amy—Georgia)

- I feel like I lose my cool more often than I'd like. (Christine—California)

- I think the biggest thing that produces guilt in me is when I get angry with my children and don't keep myself under control. I grew up in a similar situation and did not like it, so when I see myself doing the same thing, it hurts me. (Karen—Texas)

- At times I fall sooooo short of being who God wants me to be as their mother because I lose my temper or don't spend enough time just praying for them. (Diane—Minnesota)

If you are like me, we have planned and dreamed about this experience of raising children more than any other venture in life. So when we feel we are failing, the guilt comes at us in many different forms: always comparing ourselves to other moms; wishing that we, our husbands, and our children were different; and striving for perfection in *everything*. On the way to that perfection we run into time constraints, work schedules, a house to clean, and any number of other interruptions. The result of all those pressures is that anger, like a cherry on top of a sundae, finds its place on top of the pile of guilt (too bad it doesn't have the sweet aftertaste that the cherry does). And we are left to question our role as moms.

We may feel uncertainty about our performance as moms, but the truth is: We were still "meant to be moms." God didn't make a mistake when He gave you children; they were part of His plan for you. So don't worry. We are all failures at times. There will be struggles and guilt grenades along the way. But let those struggles with your children mature you rather than cause you guilt.

stop, drop, and **restore** your soul

1. What makes you feel most guilty as a mom?
2. How do you deal with the guilt you feel? How does it come out in your daily life?
3. Where does your guilt come from? (yourself, your mom, your mother-in-law, friends)
4. How has God used your failures and struggles to help you grow?

Lord,

Please give me perspective. This is a hard job, but with Your strength, not an impossible one. On those days that I'm tired, give me energy to be happy with my family. Help me, so that I don't linger in my feelings of guilt, but find hope that You have a plan for me even in my failures. Free me to live like You want me to live. Change my thoughts and desires to be true and right.

Clinging to You ... Amen.

making the **most** of the moments

1. **two-week notice** Make a list of three activities you'd like to do with your children/family within the next two weeks. Write them on specific days on the calendar, and then commit yourself to doing at least two of them before the two weeks are up.
2. **what are friends for?** Share with a friend what makes you feel most guilty. Together make a list of specific ways you are not going to allow guilt to drive your actions this week.

chapter **three**

"take your time"
Guilt Grenade #1: Lack of Family Time

I want my boys to live a simple life, and in order for that to happen, I've tried to stop running when the phone rings, or rushing out the door every time we leave. It has actually been nice for me too.
Alisha

Be still before the LORD and wait patiently for him;
do not fret—it leads only to evil.
(PSALM 37:7–8)

s we were leaving the beautiful view of Yosemite National Park, our last stop was at the park ranger's traffic booth. The kind man with his hat worn squarely on his head stepped out and said with a smile, "Take your time. Breathe the air; look at the sights; soak it all in." His purpose was to remind us to travel slowly as we made our way down the mountain road. But it struck me differently. We had just been through an enjoyable day with our family in a place God had gone full-out to create, complete with graceful yet powerful waterfalls, trees, mountains of granite, and still more waterfalls. We had "taken" our time this day. I realized as we drove away from the park ranger and the beauty behind us that it's my choice every day (not just on the easy days) to *take* the time God has given me. We take it—make the most of the moments (at bedtime, driving in the car, playing together)—or we miss it, spending time on things that really don't matter.

rocks vs. pebbles

You might have seen the illustration about putting the big rocks in the jar before you pour the pebbles in. If you pour the pebbles in first, the big rocks won't fit, overflowing out of the top of the jar. That's exactly how it is with life. If we don't commit to putting the major things into our day (time with God, investing in our families, etc.), we will be constantly chasing the small things (practices, matching stray socks) and may miss what is most important to us.

For many moms, our time is taken from us by the demands of school, extracurricular activities (ball games and music lessons), church commitments, or a job commitment, not to mention all the responsibilities a home and family bring. For single moms, your time is stretched even further, beyond your limit at times. There are more books and articles on the subject of balancing our time than there are jelly beans in a "guessing jar." But why are we trying to keep all the plates spinning at the same time? Even the trained circus performers who spend hours trying to keep the plates balanced allow one to drop on occasion!

What plates are *you* balancing? What is taking your time? What are the roles you play? It really helps to write them down—wife, mom, daughter, sister, daughter-in-law, sister-in-law, granddaughter, aunt, friend, co-worker, troop leader, moms' group leader. Now write down what each role requires of you and the time it takes. Out of those responsibilities, what are your priorities? Are you spending more time on your "most importants," those things that you'll wish you had done when your children are grown and gone? If not, what is keeping you from it? If you truly want to spend more time with your family, ask yourself what you can let go of in order to do that.

There are two areas that "steal" our time—time that could be spent with our families. If you're feeling guilty about the amount of focused time you spend (or don't spend) with your family, maybe a look at these areas will offer some ideas for helping you "take your time."

extracurricular means extra time

First, have you noticed the number of activities available for your children to participate in? T-ball, gymnastics, piano lessons, dance, soccer, to name a few, and sometimes by the ripe old age of three! And the social circles don't stop there. It seems there are more and more "positive activities" in which to involve our children. Football, basketball, cheerleading, track, golf, music lessons, chess lessons, baseball, art classes, etc. are thrown at us like this is what "normal" families do. After all, don't kids need to be "well-rounded"? That's what we're led to believe. In our society the "busy" family is often seen as the successful, normal family.

I don't know about you, but I have felt more peer pressure as a mom than I ever felt in junior high—peer pressure to have my children in activities at the expense of our family time. Here's an example: If I choose to have my three children in one competitive activity each, say cheerleading for my daughter, baseball for my son, and dance for my other daughter, that automatically means our family is involved in three separate away-from-home events. So we go to baseball practice on Monday, with a game Thursday night. Cheerleading is on Tuesday, with a competition on Saturday. Dance is at the same time the baseball game is going on, so I drop my son at his game and tell him I'll be back to pick him up—if Daddy can't make it to his game; then I take my daughter to dance. As soon as she has clicked her last clog, I hustle out the door while she hands me a note describing the special performance at a local festival on Sunday afternoon. I realize this will leave us no time to eat lunch after church; I quickly decide that sausage-on-a-stick, a staple food at festivals, must have some nutritional value. Wednesday night is Awana, leaving us hardly any nights at home for the week, with a big chunk of our weekend spoken for as well.

That frantic schedule is a scenario with just *one* activity for each kid. It is not uncommon for families to have each child involved in several activities at the same time, leaving parents in a frenzy trying to get here and there. Hurry, hurry, hurry. Rush here, rush there. Is this the lifestyle we want or the way we want our kids to live their lives? Remember, with hurry comes anger (which we'll talk about more in chapter 7).

Author Mimi Doe says, "We're giving our children too much structured time. The value of unstructured time is good. Unstructured doesn't mean unproductive."[1] As kids get older they will be able to take on more activities, but if they have participated in every sport, lesson, or class available to them by the time they turn ten, what will they have to look forward to? It's okay for kids to wait and look forward to an activity, even when their older brothers and sisters are involved in more than they are.

Most activities that children participate in require their being away from you. If they are gone to school each day and busy with after-school and weekend activities, you rarely see them. With that kind of schedule, it's no wonder fast-food restaurants are thriving. The drive-through becomes a necessity to maintain this kind of lifestyle. But kids need to have time to just play, to eat meals, and to simply hang out at home. The following questions and answers come from a magazine for single moms, but they offer sound advice that we can all learn from.

> Question: I'm a single mom (children 8 and 11). After two very hard years, I feel like I'm on the verge of losing the things most precious to me—my kids. I come in tired from work and spend most of my evening correcting them. Because money is tight, I also feel like they miss out on extracurricular activities that their friends are enjoying. I've considered taking on another job, but that would give me even less time with my kids. What can I do to replace this chaos with order?
>
> Answer: You allude to the belief that extracurricular activities measure a parent's success and children's happiness. But with this misguided emphasis, family becomes more about "doing" than "being." I've yet to counsel a person in crisis who regretted not participating in summer soccer or baseball. Yet many lament, "My parents were never there for me when I needed them." Once again, when too much "doing" gets in the way of "being a family," chaos can result. Make it a priority to spend time with your kids. Tell and show them that you are always there for them. This practice, not extracurricular activities, will make a difference in your child's life.[2]

Maybe your kids beg and plead to take part in lots of extra activities. Don't forget that you are the parent. You have to make decisions that are right for your family. Realize that it is okay to say no to some of their wants. It actually means you're being a responsible parent. If we won't allow our children to eat too much candy, it makes no sense that we would let them handle such a huge decision as what will take their time—as well as the time of the entire family.

If you find yourself running and never relaxing with your family, maybe there are some activities you could live without. Before you commit to extracurricular activities, "take your time" and evaluate how it will affect your family life.

Here's how one mom put it: "There is a pressure of sorts—that maybe the other moms won't really 'like me' if I don't 'measure up' to expectations. So . . . I remind myself that I am God's daughter, and that

I am only here to please *Him* in raising His children. I remain true to that, and I find that I am a LOT happier mommy! I don't battle the guilts of 'Oh no. . . . what if?' in every little thing" (Kelly).

The Bible says, "'Are you tired? Worn out? . . . Come to Me. Get away with me and you'll recover your life. I'll show you how to take a real rest. Walk with me and work with me—watch how I do it. Learn the unforced rhythms of grace. I won't lay anything heavy or ill-fitting on you. Keep company with me and you'll learn to live freely and lightly'" (Matthew 11:28–30 THE MESSAGE).

God's plan for us is to live freely and lightly. Even though there are inevitable responsibilities that go along with mothering, and life in general, don't let the world put those heavy, ill-fitting things on your shoulders. We have enough to carry already!

whoever said "cleanliness is next to godliness"?

The other trap that keeps moms from "taking time" with their families is the desire to have an immaculate house. Cleaning can steal not only my *time*, but also my *patience* and my *joy* as I struggle to get the family to join in my effort. I'm doing it for the family, right?

Whoever said, "Cleanliness is next to godliness"? For me, it's more like cleanliness (with children) is next to impossible! It has been said that trying to clean house with a preschooler is like shoveling snow in a snowstorm. For those of you with preschoolers, if there was ever a time to simplify your life, now is the time! Some of you with teenagers have decided it won't get much better until they leave home.

One mom who felt the exhaustion of caring for small children said, "I felt as if I was part of some odd lab experiment, the sole purpose of which was to see how physically active I could be while actually accomplishing very little!"[3]

I (Sharon) am training my children to help around the house, but it is a long, laborious, often wanna-pull-your-hair-out process. My four-year-old daughter has the job of emptying the silverware from the dishwasher. After playing with every utensil, having them talk to each other, jump in the wrong bin, then into the right one, playing like they are lost, and who knows what else, thirty minutes have come and gone! My husband confessed that he put all the silverware away himself rather than prodding and pushing her to get it done. What parent hasn't done that?

Our friend Cynthia says she has learned to lighten up and let some things go with her teens. She doesn't require them to make their beds unless someone is coming over to visit. In my family my husband and I train as we can, but it has often been more practical for me to clean up one time a day: at night when my children are sleeping. Then when we hit the floor in the morning (or more likely in the middle of the night), at least there is nothing to trip over. Sometimes I get my husband to help so we can have time together; at other times I skip it that day and we just watch our step! If you absolutely *must* have an immaculate "clean haven," consider cleaning your bedroom and keeping the door closed. It is fine to label that room "off limits" to your children so you can keep it clean.

Stephanie Nickel suggests, "Make your goal (with children) the development of good habits and a sense of shared responsibility, not an immaculate house."[4] When the goal—good habits and shared responsibility (which means you don't follow behind the kids re-cleaning what they just cleaned)—is attainable, home can be a happier, more peaceful place . . . a place you *all* want to be.

With kids you have to teach and train over and over again. Just because we tell them at breakfast doesn't mean they'll remember to take their plate to the sink after the next meal. It's the same with God and us. He has to work on me in the same areas over and over, but thankfully He doesn't give up on me. His patience helps me remember that I need to be patient when I have to ask my children for the fifth (or fiftieth) time to put away their "stuff." Maybe eventually they'll get it!

If you're like me, it's hard to slow down long enough to invest in the lives of your family, because all you can see is the pile of dirty laundry, dishes that need to be washed, bills waiting to be paid, couch cushions with stains to clean, and on and on it goes. When you catch yourself in a frantic cleaning frenzy, forgetting the feelings of your family, remember that the goal is to have a peaceful home, not a spotless one.

When you can't see above the mess, look into the eyes of your kids. Take their cheeks in your hands and look at the details of their faces. When we are caught up with cleanliness, we miss their faces. I'm just guessing, because I'm not there yet, but I'll bet one day I will miss the scattered toys, socks, paper, crayons, and dead caterpillars in the carpet, because they are evidence that children live within my walls. Lighten up about the squeaky clean house. Enjoy your children where they are. Now is the time; don't miss it. "Take your time."

"Love in the Home"

If I live in a house of spotless beauty with everything in its place,
But have not love, I am a housekeeper—not a homemaker.
If I have time for waxing, polishing, and decorative achievements,
But have not love, my children learn cleanliness—not godliness.
Love leaves the dust in search of a child's laugh.
Love smiles at the tiny fingerprints on a newly cleaned window.
Love wipes away the tears before it wipes up the spilled milk.
Love picks up the child before it picks up the toys.
Love is present through the trials.
Love reprimands, reproves, and is responsive.
Love crawls with the baby, walks with the toddler, runs with the child,
Then stands aside to let the youth walk into adulthood.
Love is the key that opens salvation's message to a child's heart.
Before I became a mother I took glory in my house of perfection.
Now I glory in God's perfection of my child.
As a mother, there is much I must teach my child,
But the greatest of all is love.
    —Author unknown[5]

stop, drop, and restore your soul

One day Laurie and I met a grandfather in McDonald's who told us, "I wish I had spent as much time with my son as I have with my grandsons." Now he had time for them, but he hadn't *made* time when his son was a boy. Quality time won't come knocking on our door. It's something we choose to pursue in spite of many distractions. It's not easy to stop our grown-up serious world to go outside and shoot hoops, have a tea party, play a board game, or wrestle on the floor. But if we don't, we risk missing the opportunity to really know our kids. It's easy to feel guilty when we look back and feel like we have already missed opportunities with our kids. But don't look back. What can you do right now, right where you are, to take the time you have, whether your kids are preschoolers, school age, teenage, or grown? Now is the time. Do what you can to "take your time" today!

1. What does "quality time" look like to you? List some of your ideas and put them on the fridge so you'll have them handy. You'll be able to turn spare time into quality time (examples: long walks, playing on the floor, family game night, quiet talks at bedtime).

2. How often are you at home as a family? What takes you away from home the most?

3. How would you describe your housecleaning style? (neat freak, clutter queen, or somewhere in the middle?)

4. How do you treat the people in your home when it is time to clean up the house? Does your view of what a house should look like consider the people, especially the children, who live there? (Some houses look as if no one really sleeps, eats, or plays there.)

5. What is it that "takes your time"? Is it something you can or cannot change? Would you like to pray about it as a family?

Lord,

Thank You for watching over my family as we go through our day. Some days are so full that I feel like we didn't live them—we endured them. Help us learn how to rest in You and enjoy our days. When we are home, Father, help us to really be together. It will be something only You can do, but please, Lord, help me to see my children's faces before I see the mess. Trim our schedule as You see fit, Lord. Give me wisdom to see things the way You would. Learning to rest . . . Amen.

making the most of the moments

1. **we are family!** Cut a piece of poster board (big or small, depending on your space to display the finished product) in as many pieces as you have members in your family. Give each person a piece of the "puzzle" and provide crayons. Everybody draw something. We had everyone draw different designs (polka

dots, shapes, squiggles, stripes). Or you could have everyone follow a theme (if your kids are old enough to follow a theme). After everyone is finished, tape the pieces back together. We're so different, but together ... we're a masterpiece! Then display your family masterpiece somewhere that you can all see it. Say together, "Families stick together in all kinds of trouble" (Proverbs 17:17b THE MESSAGE).

2. **on your mark ...** Set a timer for thirty minutes. Tell your kids that it's "Cleaning Olympics" for half an hour; then after the timer beeps, you will do something *they* want to do for thirty minutes. Give them specific jobs rather than just saying, "Clean your room." Kids work better with specific instructions, like "Put all the books away." Sometimes I tell them, "Straighten your shoes; then when you're finished with that, come ask me 'What's next?'" It gives them a sense of accomplishment, and I know the job is getting done without Mom nagging.

3. **cleaning spurts** For a quick clean-up, occupy your children with some activity, then set a timer for ten minutes. You'll be amazed at how much you can get done in ten minutes.

chapter **four**

whether i do—whether i don't

Guilt Grenade #2:
Stay-at-Home and Go-to-Work Guilt

---

*I work out of the home, which helps some, but I would
love to be all there for them. I feel like I'm doing a
halfhearted job, and that grieves me. That's where
the guilt comes from … time and patience. I know I'm
where God placed me, although sometimes it's really hard
with all there is to do and be.*

Jan

**Whatever you do, work at it with all your heart,
as working for the Lord, not for men.**

(COLOSSIANS 3:23)

When we began writing this book, there were no plans for this chapter. But when we received so much feedback about the guilt moms feel about work—from those who work outside the home and those who work at home—we knew it was something that needed to be included. Some moms feel guilty if they stay at home because they aren't helping out enough financially, and if they work outside the home, they feel guilty for not being with the family enough. How can you be a "mom and loving it" if you're always feeling guilty about where you spend your time?

Laurie and I have an unusual situation because we are *mostly* stay-at-home moms, but we also work outside the home (I guess that's obvious, since we have written this book). Our husbands are stay-at-home dads who work for the ministry, which makes ours a unique situation. We tour six-to-nine months out of the year with our families—2 moms, 2 dads, and 6 children! It takes all of us to make this lifestyle of traveling, speaking, homeschooling, and parenting work. Our work schedule is very sporadic. So it is from that perspective—sort of working part-time—that we offer these ideas. We feel that there are two main suggestions we can offer as you consider your work options.

when at home, be at home

First, **when you are with your family, be with them.** It will take discipline for stay-at-home moms to really "take time" for their children. I remember being at home with my children and realizing at the end of the day that I had not stopped once to read a book, play on the floor, or watch a PBS show with the kids. I had been cleaning, talking on the phone, or preparing meals all day. I was *there*, but I wasn't *with* them.

It will also take discipline for working moms to say no to outside activities so that their family can eat dinner at home together. Vickie, a single mom with a ten-year-old son, said that because he is her priority she doesn't make many commitments at night that take her away from him.

For working moms it's important to leave work at work. This is especially hard to do when your office is at home. After one of our programs a young mom, feeling defeated, asked, "How do you make time for your kids when you are running a home business?" I acknowledged the challenge of "working at home" and suggested that she try doing as much work during naptime as possible and designating a specific "quitting time." It helps to set time limits and stick to them. When the quitting time comes you have to be disciplined enough to wrap it up! Then for thirty minutes, do what your child wants to do. If necessary, ask a young neighbor girl (maybe an eight- to ten-year-old) to come over after school a few days per week to help entertain your children while you get another hour or two of work done.

Our mom worked all of our lives, but I never felt like Mom's work came before us. When she came home, she was home, and she loved being home. She was like a super-mom (if I compare myself to her I'll start feeling guilty again); she sewed for us, made great birthday cakes, had a garden, prepared home-cooked meals, canned, cleaned, loved our dad, almost always had people over for Sunday lunch, cared for elderly people, and even found the time to disciple me as a new Christian (I'll stop now, so you won't start to feel guilty too). The point I'm making isn't that we should be a super-mom. God gifted my mom in different areas than He gifted me. What I do want to stress is that our mom, as a full-time working mom, left her work at work, and when she was with us, *she was really with us*. Whether you work at home or away, when you are with your children, resist the temptation to allow distractions to keep you from really being with them.

am i where God wants me to be?

The second point to consider has to do with calling. The most important question to ask yourself is **"Am I really doing what God wants me to do?"** Notice we didn't say, "what other people want me to do"; God is the One who matters most. Proverbs 16:9 (paraphrased) says, "In her heart a woman plans her course, but the Lord determines her steps." If you feel you're doing what God wants you to do, rest in His peace. "A heart at peace gives life to the body" (Proverbs 14:30). What mom doesn't need peace that will give life to her body?

Many moms struggle with guilt about their working situations. Some stay-at-home moms question what has happened to their life now that the "pats on the back" they once received at work have disappeared. One mom (Janet) said, "I went from a highly paid, fearfully respected executive . . . to a morbidly underpaid stay-at-home mom who wonders about her worth at times. I love my life, but Lord knows, I have my moments of self-doubt."

Being a stay-at-home mom takes some getting used to, some growing into. If you worked up until the time you had children, think of it this way—you are completely changing careers, without any training. Maybe you are thinking *I'm not cut out for this* because you are having a hard time adjusting. Please don't go back to work too quickly. Give it time. If you are a mom who stays at home and you don't feel comfortable, hang in there. It can take a year or more to adjust to your career change. Embrace where you are and give it some time. My husband reminded me (Sharon) that for our whole life most of us haven't spent many whole days at home. So it's no wonder that we feel some culture shock. It's a brand-new experience.

Some moms feel guilty for not helping out financially and will try to figure out every possible way to bring in cash to help pay the bills. But even in the hard times, lots of moms decide to deal with the skinny bank accounts and embrace the huge career change to be home with their kids.

It's sometimes frustrating to know that money is really, really tight, but I'm able to be home with my kids. This summer is my first true summer off since we've had kids (eight years), and we're going to the library, playing with friends, and going swimming. I still struggle with not having enough money (sometimes there's hardly enough for groceries), but I truly feel that God has given me this opportunity to be home with my kids while they're young. (Tammy)

I always knew that I wanted children. I was an "older" mom. I was thirty-six when I had my first child, so I was well into my career. I thought that I would take some extended leave and then return to work. The closer it came to the time that I had to return to work the more I realized that I wasn't a career woman. I was a MOM! I did have to return to work full-time after four months at home with my new angel. We hired a nanny so that we didn't have to wake our daughter and drag her out in the early morning hours to a day-care center. We thought this would be the best alternative. However, I cried every day when I left, and I called home many times during the day to see how my little girl was doing. This lasted six weeks before my husband and I could make arrangements for me to be home. I did have to work part-time, but I worked in the evening when my husband was home. This arrangement has worked for us now for seven years. Having me work part-time has given him the opportunity to see what's involved with being Mom! The kids enjoy their time with him and I love being home with them. We have three children now, ages seven, six, and four. Who am I? I'm Mom! (Kathleen)

It's easy to feel guilty about our situation, but one mom shared about gaining freedom from the guilt.

I've gone through seasons of contentment and restlessness. I sway from being elated over the ability to stay at home with my kids to asking myself, "What am I doing with my life to make a difference in the world?" However, I have recently found freedom from the revelation that God doesn't care about what we do. He cares about who we are. He is interested not in our doing but in our becoming. (Jennifer)

"Guilt is banished through love and truth."
(Proverbs 16:6 THE MESSAGE)

Moms who work away from the home are constantly telling us that the biggest struggle for them is balancing everything; most feel they don't spend enough time with their kids. "As a working mom, it seems that others spend more time with my child than I do. I think God has helped me keep the big picture in mind and continues to remind me to make the most out of the time we do have together." (Alisha)

It's always good to consider your options when you are trying to decide exactly what God wants you to do. If you're a working mom, in order to keep family a priority you could consider taking a lower-paying job that is closer to home. Or maybe there is a job with more flexible hours to better accommodate your kids' school schedule. Even though our mom worked outside the home, her job was very flexible and allowed her to attend our school activities and stay home with us when we were sick. (It helps when your employer values family.)

One of the songs on our album, "My Prayer," was written for moms who work outside the home. But the more we've listened to it, the more the words seem to offer hope to all of us. Though our circumstances may be different—single or married, a stay-at-home mom or a mom who goes out to work—our love for our children is the same. Ask God for His help and His wisdom about your situation. When we are weak and exhausted, He remains faithful and strong.

"My Prayer"

Here I am again, Lord, bowing down before You,
asking You to help me out somehow.
God, You say You know my thoughts before I even speak them,
so You know just what I'm thinking now.
I am tired and oh, so weary.
Renew my strength, renew my strength.
For when I'm weak You say that You will be strong
and I need Your strength to help me carry on.
They greet me at the door with pictures that they've colored.

With excitement in their eyes they say, "Let's play."
I feel a tinge of guilt knowing I am so exhausted.
The best of me has been spent throughout the day.
I am tired and oh, so weary.
Renew my strength, renew my strength.
For when I'm weak, You say that You will be strong
and I need Your strength to help me carry on.
(Music and lyrics by Laurie Hilliard, 2MOMS,
Hold You, Mommy, copyright 1999,
www.momandlovingit.org)

Ask God for His help and then don't be afraid to trust Him. He knows every detail of your situation and cares deeply for you and for your family. He has a plan for you, and in that plan one of His primary purposes for you is being a mom. That is no small job, so seek Him as you decide what is best for your family. The sacrifices you make now to be available for your kids are decisions you'll *never* regret.

stop, drop, and restore your soul

Children are only children once. Each day is one less on the calendar of their life in our home. It's worth our consideration to determine whether or not we are doing what God wants us to do when it comes to being a stay-at-home mom or a mom who works outside the home. It's important that you do what your family needs, not what everybody else is doing. If you are questioning your work situation, ask God to show you how He feels about it. Sometimes our questions aren't resolved until we step out and trust Him to show us the way and take care of us.

1. How would you rate your satisfaction with your work arrangement right now (whether working outside the home or working as a stay-at-home mom)?
   1 = horrible, 10 = 100% satisfied
2. Do you feel like you're doing what God wants you to do? How do you know?
3. If you work outside the home and you are dissatisfied, what do you feel is the worst part about working?
4. If you are dissatisfied about staying at home, what is the worst part for you?

5. None of us wants to look back someday and say, "I missed it."
   What changes do you need to make now to avoid having
   regrets later?

Lord,

I want to be where You want me to be, but sometimes I'm confused
about where that is. Please make it clear to me. I want to be there for my
children. Give me creative ways to be there. Help them to feel like I was there
when they needed me. Give us a bond strong enough to weather the storms
of life together. Show me how to be their mom. I want to know them more
and more so I can understand what makes them tick. Here I am, Lord. Give
me the courage to trust that You know what is best for our family. Father,
giver of life, help me use the life You gave me to bless the lives of my children.
Trusting You … Amen.

making the most of the moments

Here are five ways to use your five senses to really *be with* your kids
when you're with them.

1. **seeing** Have your child/children lie down on the floor. Look at
   their faces upside down, observing until their faces look distorted. It starts looking like they have no nose or mouth. I
   know it's freaky, but kids like freaky!

2. **hearing** Lie in bed with them at night and listen together. What
   sounds make your house your home? Then listen if they want
   to talk.

3. **smelling** Do you wear a certain perfume? Spray it on before you
   hug your kids good-bye when you are going to be away from
   each other for a while. They will think of you when they smell
   it. Find a fragrance you like and stick with it. Forever it will
   remind them of Mom!

4. **touching** Hold hands when you pray. Hug and tell them you are
   so thankful God gave them to you.

5. **tasting** Have everyone pick their favorite meal just so you know.
   Then when you fix that meal, they'll know you were thinking
   specifically about them.

chapter five

angry ... and hating it!

Guilt Grenade #3: Dealing With Angry Outbursts

*When we're in the pressure cooker of the moment and
realize we're reacting rather than acting wisely, we feel bad.*
Jan

In your anger do not sin.

(EPHESIANS 4:26)

I (Sharon) sat in church that Sunday morning, sang the songs, listened to the sermon, then as the final music played, I knew I needed to pray. It was as if the Lord had set His hand on my head and said, "Today is the day we are going to deal with this." I knelt at the prayer altar and my heart was flooded with emotions. I knew immediately that God was concerned with my angry heart. Why did I have to blow up at my husband and kids?

I had been a very positive person my whole life. I had grown up in a calm home, without yelling, so where was this harshness I heard in my voice and hardness I saw on my face coming from? It was an anger I hadn't really seen until I married and had children. The people I loved the most I treated the worst. Maybe my husband was a little later getting home than he thought or the kids forgot to wipe their feet—again. Small things would throw me into a frenzy. Sometimes I could blame it on that monthly occurrence, but sometimes there was no reasonable explanation.

On my knees, through tears of anguish, I asked God to forgive me. I realized it was a sin to treat others so harshly, especially those I loved dearly. But I knew that God would forgive anything and that included my hurtful words toward my family. "If we confess our sins, he is faithful and just and will forgive us our sins and purify us from all unrighteous-ness" (1 John 1:9).

After asking God's forgiveness I committed myself to asking my family to forgive me as well. Before I stood to my feet, I asked God, "Please help me think what my words will sound like before I speak them and what my face will look like before I look a certain way." With that prayer and the forgiveness I felt, I had hope. I asked my husband and children to forgive me, and we moved on. I was sure I was cured.

Two weeks passed and I was doing good. I mean, God was doing good! Yeah, that's right. It was God. He had been faithful to answer my prayer and help me to be more positive—more of a cheerleader than a naysayer. In all honesty, I was pretty proud of what *I* had done, that *I* had made a change, that *I* was different. Pride really does come before a fall (Proverbs 16:18).

One day I was rushing out the door with my children. I loaded one into her car seat, then discovered that the oldest (who was four) had decided it was time she learned to drive. I asked her to move back to her seat, to which she replied (to my surprise), "No." It wasn't an ugly, nose-crinkled, mouth-pursed no. It was more a flippant no that said, "I think I'll drive today since I can't even see over the dashboard." I calmly lifted her back to her seat, which made this strong-willed child very angry. If I wouldn't let her push the pedals, at least I should let her sit in my lap and steer! I went around to buckle her seat belt despite the screaming and crying. (It was that fake crying that moms can see right through.) I shut the door, walked around the car, trying to stay in control, pulled the door handle to get in, only to find that my little angel had locked the door while sitting in my seat. As soon as she realized I was locked out and she had done it, her phony crying turned to hysterical laughter. (Do you ever feel like kids are spies in miniature, seeking to find the magic buttons that will make us explode?) Thankfully, I had my key—and didn't break it off in the keyhole as I furiously tried to open the door. I thought, *Doesn't she realize that we're already late? All her clowning around is just going to make me have to drive faster. If I get a ticket—!*

As I struggled to open the door, God was gently reminding me, "Remember, it will sound really harsh if you lay into her. You might want to check your face in the rearview mirror before you back out of the driveway." He was reminding me, but did I listen? Hah! I finally jerked the door open, then tore into her like a dog fighting with a piece of paper. "Listen to me, young lady! You had better be faster about obeying next time. When I tell you to move, you move! I can't believe you would be so insensitive and make us late" (now all the rushing is her fault!) "when you knew we were in a hurry. You'd better straighten up, sister, or things aren't going to be very fun for you!" And with that, like Mr. Potato Head putting on his angry eyes, I glared at my four-year-old (that I was treating like a sixteen-year-old) in the rearview mirror with harsh, demeaning eyes to find that now the tears were real.

As we drove on, the only sound was the baby babbling. Guilt poured over me like someone had cracked a dozen eggs on my head. I realized I had done it again—I wasn't 100 percent cured. I silently asked God to forgive me—again—then glanced at my daughter's tearstained face and asked her to forgive me. "Brittlea, I was wrong to talk to you that way. I was harsh and cruel. Would you please forgive me?" She softly said, "Yes, Mommy, but you scared me."

I was crushed. *What kind of mom,* I thought, *would be so insensitive as to scare her daughter?* This was not what I had envisioned myself to be as a mom. Moms who scared their children, in my mind, always lived in another city or state. It was hard for me to realize that one of these moms lived in the house with my children! I was thirty years old and she was four! How could I let her get to me this way? Why couldn't I be the adult?

My string of self-condemning thoughts led me to remember that I had asked God's forgiveness, and my daughter had forgiven me. Now it was my turn to forgive myself. For most people, the hardest person to forgive is yourself. I usually say, "Sharon, I forgive you for yelling at your daughter. You are not perfect, and God knows that. But He hasn't given up on you, so don't give up on yourself. He is growing you to be more like Him even when you mess up." I used to make fun of women who talked to themselves. Now I'm right up there with the best of them!

After this incident I thought about my misconception . . . that I had changed immediately. There are some things that *do* change overnight—Jell-O, for example. But just as children don't grow into adults overnight, it takes time for God to change habits and emotions in us as well. He is capable of changing us immediately, but usually He wants us to learn through the process of change. On my knees that day in church, I thought God had miraculously taken my anger problem away. But He hadn't. What He had done was start the process of changing me.

I'm not totally over my anger, but I can see a big difference since that time. Now I have another area that God is working on, but knowing that He has changed me before helps me to trust Him with this new area as well. He is always looking for ways to help me become more like Jesus. Some people have personal fitness trainers. As Christians we have a personal spiritual trainer who is on our side, watching for ways to help us grow. Often He uses our relationships, especially the ones with our children and mates, to grow our spiritual muscles.

anger is normal

"Anger is basically a God-given physical response to a perceived threat. It's part of the way we're made, and we can't help feeling it from time to time."[1] Even Jesus got angry. When the temple was being used more as a mall than a place to worship God, He was angry. (See Matthew 21:12–14.) So it's not anger in itself that should make us feel guilty. Usually my guilt comes from knowing I'm upset about something trivial, like my husband's driving habits or the constant giggling of my children. (Shouldn't I be glad they're not fussing?)

Anger is normal, but . . . when does it cross over into the area of being sin? When our anger causes unnecessary, undeserved hurt it becomes sin. When our anger becomes selfish—"How dare you make me look like a bad mother in front of my friends?"—or when we are abusing another person physically, verbally, or emotionally, we've crossed the sin line.

If you've done this, don't despair. You're not the first one. But get some help from someone you trust—perhaps your pastor or a good friend. Living with constant guilt won't eliminate the problem; it could actually intensify your anger. If you grew up in a home with abuse, it would be hard for you to know how a godly, healthy family functions. Find a family that you admire and ask them what they do in certain situations. If you can, spend time with them to help you get on the right track. No one is hopeless. The Lord can help you learn new patterns of behavior that will benefit everyone in your family.

trouble spots

What causes our anger and what can we do to prevent hurting those we love by our harsh responses? There are lots of things that can make us "lose it" with our husband and kids. But two of the most common are:

- dealing with things out of our control; and
- always being in a hurry.

dealing with the unexpected

There are lots of unexpected things that happen in a mom's life, like fingernail polish remover being spilled all over brand-new carpet. One time when my daughter was being potty trained and before I (Sharon) could get her in a diaper, she hid in my closet and pooped, then stepped in it—and made her way across the carpet to the kitchen. Kids do unexpected things—that just goes with the territory.

My four-year-old asked for a crayon, but evidently didn't have paper. I must have been preoccupied and handed her the crayon without paying much attention. So she proceeded to write on the door of the van—the rental van. I disciplined her and made her scrub the door. I talked to her about why she did it. She didn't know. (Of course! Why would I even ask? What's she going to say? "Mom, I felt that I needed to color on the pretty rental van because the next person would see the marks and be thankful God put children on the earth"? Ha!) So I told her when she was tempted to do something she knew was wrong to tell me.

When we got in the van again, she found a pen and did the same thing! (Don't you think they do things sometimes just to see us blow our top?) We scrubbed and spanked again. I talked with her about being tempted and asking for help, fleeing temptation instead of running toward it. On the plane that day, she was sitting next to me when suddenly this child who normally thinks milk is "good to the last drop," handed me her half-full milk carton. I asked if she was finished and she said, "I'm feeling like I want to spit it." She was tempted and she told me—Yea! (Sharon)

Moms have experiences every day that make them want to rejoice—or pull their hair out! "Moms, more than just about any other category of human beings, are the most likely to battle anger, for many reasons. For one, we live so constantly with moments that are out of our control."[2]

we're in a hurry!

The other easy-to-recognize cause of angry outbursts is being in too much of a hurry. Remember my story about losing it with my daughter? "I was rushing out the door . . ." What does rushing do? It causes panic. When you and I are in a hurry it's hard to think about other people, especially those children in your life who piddle! So, I'm learning that if I'm in a hurry, I need to be aware of the pit bull in me that can get loose at any time.

Two chapters ago, we talked about being so busy that you don't have time to be at home. Being less busy will also help you to be less angry. Busy makes your adrenaline rush and your blood boil. Those are things you'd rather save for those emergency trips to the hospital. But when you do have to hurry (and of course we all will), or when unexpected disasters occur, how can we handle it in a more positive way?

diffusing angry outbursts

- **Pray!** I am very familiar with the prayer I mentioned early in this chapter, "Lord, help me think before something ugly comes out of my mouth or before I look disgustedly at my children or husband." The best way I know how to ward off unwanted anger is to seek God's help.

- **Laugh Instead of Cry** I've found that for those unexpected things, those things that really were accidents, we are all better off if we can laugh instead of cry. To laugh is contrary to what we feel like doing and is often not what we experienced growing up. When I realized that there was poop all over the floor, I could have cried and thrown a fit, but what good would that have done? Instead, I laughed. It *was* funny, really. Why wait and laugh about it in a few years? Save yourself the guilt of being angry and just laugh. Not that I haven't cried and thrown a fit on occasion—the fingernail polish remover spilled on new carpet was one time I lost it. The difference in that situation was that she (the offender) knew not to

have any product with the word "fingernail" on the label anywhere near the carpet. She just chose to ignore the rules. I wasn't
abusive in my anger, but she knew Momma was serious, and we
haven't had a problem since. You can't laugh about everything, but
when you can, let loose!

• **Avoid Frustrating Situations When Possible** I know you are
thinking, *Well, duh, if I could always do that then I'd never have a
reason to be angry.* What I mean is, try to identify what situations
during the day repeatedly make you want to scream and see what
can be done on your part to understand and change them.

My cousin, who has four kids, told me (Laurie) that she gets angry
with her kids primarily for two reasons: when they interrupt her agenda/
plans, and when they inconvenience her. Unfortunately, God didn't
promise that children would always be convenient! Part of our job
description as moms is to anticipate interruptions in our days.

I love Sally Clarkson's view of embracing God's call of motherhood:

Instead of seeing fusses and messes as irritations in my day . . . I
am more likely to see them as opportunities to train my children to
be peacemakers and to learn to be responsible for their own messes.
Instead of resenting the interruptions in my schedule, I am more
likely to accept them as divine appointments. More and more, I have
learned to see my children through the eyes of God and to accept the
stages of growth through which He has designed them to grow.[3]

I have found that the root of my frustration is not always about my
children interrupting me, even though initially I may think it is. Sometimes the aggravating situation could have been avoided had I planned
ahead a little better.

For example, bedtime can be a struggle for many moms. Our bedtime routine—or the lack thereof—can make me crazy. I get very cranky
when my kids lollygag when they are supposed to be getting ready for
bed (especially when I'm in a hurry). I am usually so tired that all I can
think about is having time alone as soon as they are asleep! I longed for
our bedtime routine to be a peaceful, enjoyable family time, but instead
it was a chaotic, frustrating, exhausting time.

The truth is, our bedtime chaos wasn't entirely my kids' fault. I realized that this was a situation that *could be avoided* if I would start the process of going to bed earlier. It was hard for me to comprehend how early I actually had to begin the "going to bed" process. Here is the schedule that works well in our house. Your schedule will vary depending on the age of your children, but it sometimes helps to see an example in print.

Bedtime Routine

All homework done by 6:00
6:00 Dinner—(don't wash the dishes yet)
6:45 Baths (don't try to get other things done. Make the kids your focus or you will get distracted and so will your children)
7:15 Brush teeth/get water/go to the bathroom/get pj's on
7:30 Kids get in bed—read, pray, and talk (probably they will go to the bathroom, again)
8:00 Bedtime routine is done. Lights out.
8:30 Everyone is asleep (hopefully!) and Mom has her time.

All my children (except the three-year-old) are old enough to get their own water before bed, brush their own teeth, and put their pj's on. I have found that the process of brushing their teeth goes much more quickly if I send one kid to the bathroom at a time. Before, I would tell them "Hey kids, go brush your teeth." They would all gallop to the bathroom at the same time, fight over the toothpaste, the sink, and "their turn." It would become an absolute fiasco, with me in the middle trying to referee the wrestling match. Now I send them one by one to avoid the problem altogether.

You might even set a timer and give them fifteen minutes (or less) to get everything done. Then make it a game for them to be in bed before the timer goes off. If my desired bedtime for them is 8:30, then I need to have the timer go off at 8:00. This gives us time to read together, pray, give hugs and kisses, and maybe answer all the "last questions" of the day.

I know this is no guarantee that all will go well, but at least the chances for a peaceful bedtime are greatly improved. I wasn't as angry and rushed getting them ready for bed, and whenever they did finally go to sleep, it was earlier than previous nights because we started earlier. I can live with that!

say no with a smile

One Friday night my daughter and I (Sharon) were driving to a football game to watch my husband's band perform. (He was the high school band director for our school.) On the way we stopped for ice cream. I was proud of myself for letting her have ice cream, knowing that she might have it all down her front before we got to the game. When we arrived at the game we headed to the concession stand to pick up a drink for my husband (who hadn't had ice cream before the game).

As is common at all concession stands in America, I suppose, the candy was lined up on the counter, eye level for every four-year-old who walks up. My daughter spied the candy and started the process: ask, ask again, ask some more, and finally, when all else fails, keep asking! With a frown on my face, I answered, "Honey, we just had ice cream fifteen minutes ago."

There was an elderly gentleman behind the counter, a member of the Lions Club, who heard our conversation and said, "Ohhh . . . 'No' goes over so much better with a smile." I stood there stunned for a moment, wondering where he had come from and who asked him for help anyway! I was tugged back to reality by my daughter's yank on my pants and her now manipulative manner of asking, "Mommy, look, they have Skittles. I haven't had any of those in a long time. Can I have some? I like Milky Way too." I looked down at her with my newfound advice in mind and said with a smile, "Honey, remember, we just had ice cream." She laughed and said, "Oh, yeah!" End of questions! The man looked at me, grinned, and said, "See!" I was amazed. Saying no with a smile is a great way to prevent an angry outburst.

As moms there are tons of things that can light our fire. But there are ways we can throw water on the fire before it starts blazing: By being less busy so we aren't always in a hurry, asking God to help us think about what it will sound like before the words leave our mouth, praying, laughing instead of crying, and saying no with a smile. Those tools are sort of like mental fire extinguishers! We can't eliminate the struggles, but we can minimize the hurt we cause others by using these tools to soften our responses.

stop, drop, and restore your soul

Kids bring such joy, but they can also bring stress. Is that part of God's plan to see us grow? Absolutely! We can fight the process or embrace it and learn.

1. Do you get angry with your kids or your husband? (Just say yes!)
2. What makes you angry?
3. Describe a frustrating time in your day (dinnertime, bedtime, homework time, morning time). How can you possibly avoid some of the frustration of that time? What are some changes you could make that might help?
4. How do you usually handle your anger in public? How do you express your anger in the privacy of your home?
5. Which one of the suggestions to diffuse angry outbursts would be best for you to incorporate into your life? How would it help you soften your responses?

Lord,

   We love our kids so much, but they can make us so mad at times! I know You made them and understand them. Help us respond to them the way You want us to and the way they need us to respond. Soften our words. Help us to think before we speak, to laugh instead of cry, to smile more even when we have to say no. We ask Your forgiveness for the times we've lost it in the past. Free us from the guilt that our sin has heaped upon our heads. Wash us and make us clean. Thank You for Your faithfulness. In Jesus' name. Amen.

"Because of the LORD's great love we are not consumed, for his compassions never fail. They are new every morning; great is your faithfulness" (Lamentations 3:22–23).

making the most of the moments

1. **just yell it!** Go outside and just yell ... altogether ... yell. Boys will really love this. When we were kids our brother would go outside and just scream, not because he was angry, but he was

just getting it out, whatever "it" was. People might think you're weird, but kids love it when their parents loosen up and have fun!

2. **mirror, mirror, on the wall** Go to a mirror and look at your face. Do you have a constant frown? Say the word *no* while looking in the mirror. Then say it while smiling. Now, was that so hard? Practice smiling the next time you tell your child no.

3. **please forgive me** If you have been verbally cruel or physically abusive in your anger toward your children (or a spouse), ask them for forgiveness. Next, find a girl friend with whom you can share everything ... I mean everything. Ask her to hold you accountable regarding your anger. Then pray and ask God to help you change.

chapter **six**

finding true contentment
in life

Every Mom's Greatest Hope

---

*I realized just how much God loves us. I never knew the
true depth of His love until I had our first child. I then
understood unconditional love and what it meant
to be a child of God.*

Ann

*I know what it is to be in need, and I know what it is to have
plenty. I have learned the secret of being content in any and every
situation, whether well fed or hungry, whether living in plenty or in
want. I can do everything through him who gives me strength.*

(PHILIPPIANS 4:12–13)

My friend Janie has the best attitude. I (Sharon) don't think I've ever heard her complain. She's always got an encouraging word to share and would never intentionally offend anyone. She keeps up with my birthday as well as other special events in my life, sending notes that are both uplifting and challenging. In one of her notes she wrote, "The joy and memories that you've made during these days are treasures more valuable than gold" (Matthew 6:19–21). She reminded me, "Lean on the Lord, having no doubts of His love for you" (Romans 8:38–39).

I've kept that letter in my bathroom for over a year, just so I could be reminded to lean on the Lord each day as I opened my medicine cabinet. Janie diligently studies God's Word, encourages others with His Word, lives a life that shines with contentment, and has a face that is radiant. She has a smile that won't quit and a laugh that is so sincere it makes her eyes squint.

Janie is that friend you could call who would be there no matter what, the friend that would do anything for you—at least anything that her wheelchair would allow. You see, she was born with cerebral palsy, a condition that has kept her from walking her whole life and forced her to be dependent on others for even the simplest things. She's never been married and has no children. So how can she be so content?

the world's solutions for finding contentment

I've often heard two pieces of advice given on talk shows, at church, and friend to friend about how to make yourself feel better, how to be more content. The first cure for discontentment goes something like this:

1. Look around; when you do, you'll always find someone who is worse off than yourself. That will help you have a thankful heart.

I've tried this strategy, sort of "guilting" myself into a thankful heart. It doesn't take long for me to find someone who has less money, a harder life, an unhappy marriage, a smaller house, or physical attributes that aren't particularly desirable. For a while it works, but those "good, thankful" feelings only last until I look outside of myself and see someone else whose situation is *better* than my own. Then it's easy to be envious and discontented all over again.

Another popular cure for gaining contentment with yourself is to simply:

2. Be positive.

There is nothing wrong with positive self-talk. Many times it's a choice we have to make, but being positive isn't the final cure. There are some days that I can stay upbeat, but other days fatigue, the weight of responsibility, and certain times of the month can steal my ability to see anything positive in my circumstances.

janie's contentment

Janie has a thankful heart and an incredibly positive outlook on life, but she didn't become that way by finding someone worse off than herself or by just being positive. Her reasons for being content in her circumstances are by-products of the strength she finds in Christ. She has a personal relationship with Jesus Christ, which began on April 23, 1978 (the same day I started my relationship with Him), and from that time till now she has depended on Him and has grown to love Him with her whole heart, soul, mind, and strength.

There is no other solution that can give you the ability to have a foundation of thankfulness—regardless of your situation or circumstances. Because of Christ, Janie has a grateful heart and a positive attitude that make her radiant even in her confinement.

So it doesn't really matter what our circumstances are. We opened this chapter with the Scripture written by Paul in Philippians 4:12–13. Paul said he had learned to be content in every circumstance; he knew what it was like to be in need and to have plenty. Sometimes as a struggling mom, I think, "Good for you, Paul, 'cause I'm not there!"

Paul's statement "I have learned the secret of being content" is truly amazing when you find out what Paul actually went through. He was whipped, beaten with rods, stoned, imprisoned, shipwrecked three times, and spent a day and night in the open sea—not exactly favorable circumstances by anyone's standards! (See 2 Corinthians 11:24–27.)

What was the secret he learned? In the next verse he says, "I can do everything through him who gives me strength." *The Message* says it like this (v. 13): "Whatever I have, wherever I am, I can make it through anything in the One who makes me who I am." Paul realized that his ability to be content came as a result of his strength through Christ, not because of himself or his circumstances, not because of positive self-talk or finding someone in a situation worse than his own.

You might ask, "As a mom, why do I need Jesus?" One mom said,

> About a year ago I was completely exhausted from the quandary of *who am I* when all of the important people in my life needed me to be something different. I joined a small group Bible study and really started focusing major attention on my relationship with the Lord, and in that still, quiet voice, He reminded me of who I really am: His child. Now I bring that to all five of the wonderful blessings in my life, and I've found that I don't have to change who I am to meet their needs . . . God just meets their needs through me! (Suzanne)

When your strength runs out you can lean on His strength. Lean on Him and never doubt His love for you. The key is not a religion; it's a real *relationship* with Jesus. If you go to church and just go through the motions He is not real to you. He can't do anything for you because you aren't truly trusting Him with your life.

the hope for all of us

I don't share about Janie to make you feel sorry for her—that's really the last thing she would want. And I don't share her story with you to show you there are people who are worse off than you, and so "shape up and be thankful." Those are hollow solutions.

I share the story of Janie because her life illustrates the key to contentment. Everything the world says should make you happy *she doesn't have*. Without the hope she has in Jesus she could be miserable: mad that the rest of the world gets to have families of their own, frustrated that she can't "go" to work, angry that walking was something she was never able to enjoy. But because of Christ, she has a hope and a future. She knows that God wouldn't have put her here if her life was meaningless.

Because of her faith in Him she knows she has a purpose, just like every person has—including you and me. She is living that purpose too, through her writing. She doesn't just write notes to encourage friends. God has given her the opportunity to change lives through her writing. (For more information about her book of poetry, see Appendix 1 under "Other Resources.") That is her gift. She would tell you that she does have hard days—days of wishing things could be different, days she cries, and days of pain, but her foundation—the foundation that is stronger than any two legs could ever be—is Christ.

leaning on Jesus

That same hope is available for all of us. Did you know that God thought through every day of your life *before* you were born? His ability to care about our days is a hard thing for us to fathom. But, think about this: Even though God created the majestic mountains He also fashioned the detailed leaves and ladybugs. He is mighty, yet He cares about the miniscule.

What's more, He sent His Son Jesus to earth to live as a human. Not as an angel, but as a human, to let us know He really does understand our thoughts and emotions in a personal way. Then, after Jesus had lived a life without ever messing up (He never had even one bad thought), He died to take care of all of our sins—*all* the bad thoughts and terrible things we have done. When He came back to life after three days, it was God's way of saying that our sins had died, but He was back!

Another amazing thing about God is that He loves you and me enough that He would never force us to love Him. He doesn't make us choose Him or force us to believe that He sent His Son for us. He wants choosing Him to be our own decision.

But why wouldn't we? It's like He has offered us a priceless gift that is just outside the front door, waiting to be opened, and yet we can choose to leave it untouched . . . unopened.

starting a relationship with Him

Starting a relationship with Jesus Christ is the first step to being content in real life. If you want to know Him personally and accept His free gift of grace and mercy; if you want to have the assurance of living with Him in heaven after you die and experience joy on earth that can outweigh your circumstances, I encourage you to invite Him into your life right now. It's not hard. Begin by praying this simple prayer.

> *Jesus, I know I need You. I can't carry on with life on my own. I have done so many things wrong; I've sinned. Please forgive me for those sins. I invite You to come into my heart and make me new. Thank You for forgiving me and for the promise of living in heaven forever someday. Help me learn to walk with You each day. In Jesus' name I pray. Amen.*

If you prayed that prayer, congratulations! You've been adopted into the biggest family ever. When I began my relationship with Christ, I remember several people telling me I had just made the biggest decision of my life. They were right. Marriage was big, and having children was huge, but this decision will affect you and me for eternity.

If you recently asked Jesus into your heart or even if you've known Him for a long time, you might have questions like "How do I know I'm really a Christian?" or "Why do I still sin, if I'm a Christian?" Just as there is much to learn about our children, there is more than a lifetime of things to learn about God. Studying about Him by reading His

Word—the Bible—helps you live more like Him. You might find a women's Bible study and join in. We have also put some information in Appendix two to help answer a few of the questions you might have to help get you started in your relationship with Him.

Getting to know God takes time. But the point is not to be legalistic and feel guilty when you miss a day's quiet time with Him. Just know that when you don't take the time for Him you are missing out on a tremendous blessing that will enrich your life. I haven't spent focused time with Him every day, especially since I became a mom, but I try not to miss those times, because they have become *so important* to me. Spending time getting to know God is something that you will never regret.

stop, drop, and restore your soul

Did you know that God knows how many hairs you have on your head? (See Luke 12:7.) Do you care how many hairs you have on your head? I don't. But God cares about the little things in our lives. He cares that you need a good parking space at Wal-Mart when you have small children, or that you want your child to hit the ball instead of striking out, *again*. He cares about it all—relationships with our husbands, children, in-laws, friends, co-workers. Talk to Him about *anything that concerns you*. Thank Him for what He has done for you. (I really do pray for a parking place at Wal-Mart, and you would be amazed at the spots He has provided.) When we trust him with the little things it's easier for us to see His answers to the bigger problems in our lives.

1. When you find someone in a situation worse than your own, how long does your "thankful heart" last?
2. How does the statement "just be positive" make you feel as a suggestion for contentment?
3. What are your thoughts about having or needing a relationship with Jesus?
4. What are some things you've been worrying about? Have you prayed and asked for God's direction in these areas?

Lord,

You know every problem I've faced, every disappointment, every person who has caused me pain. You understand my situation better than I do. Draw me to Your side, Father. Everything that has happened in my life hasn't been good, but You promise that all things will work into something good. Help me to see Your plan for my life. Thank You for making me a priority, for planning my life before my parents knew I was part of the plan. Help me live my life, not in my own strength, but in Yours. I want to depend on You, not the ideas the world offers. Help me grow to love You more and more every day. Thank You for washing away all the sins I've committed, even the ones I would be ashamed to tell anyone about. Thank You for giving me life. It's because of You, Jesus, that I have hope. In Your name I pray. Amen.

making the most of the moments

1. **getting to know God** One of the best ways to make the most of the moments in your life is to spend some of those minutes getting to know God. One mom shared: "Once I had children, my daily quiet time became extremely important. It is at that time in the morning that I can focus my thoughts, prepare for the day, ask God for help and wisdom. I need His help every day, and in drawing closer to Him, I am more content" (Michelle). How do you do that? Here are some ideas for you to try (we would never expect a busy mom to do them all).

   A. When you go walking, pray—thank God for all He has done and ask Him to forgive you for anything that you know is a sin. Talk to Him about your concerns and requests. You can talk to Him all day long about what worries you, what makes you happy, sad, or exhausted. You have a constant companion, a friend who loves to share it all with you. He is the perfect friend!

   B. Read God's Word. Read by yourself if you can; but even if you're reading your kids a Bible story, ask God to open your heart to hear what He wants to say to you. He can speak loudly through those stories!

   C. Sometimes reading a book (like you're doing right now)

can be part of your quiet time with the Lord. Using a devotional book or Bible study can keep you on track and focused on a particular area.

2. **e-mail us!!** If you invited Jesus to come into your life, we would love to know. You can e-mail us at *mail@momandlovingit.org*. Blessings!

chapter Seven

being content with who you are
Comparing: The Seed of Discontentment

Don't we all have a mommy friend who seems to "do it all" ... while making an afghan out of a cotton ball and a toothpick? We need to realize God gives us all gifts, and not to feel like we are constantly falling behind.

Janet

We're not ... putting ourselves in a league with those who boast that they're our superiors. We wouldn't dare do that. But in all this comparing and grading and competing, they quite miss the point.... What you say about yourself means nothing in God's work. It's what God says about you that makes the difference.

(2 CORINTHIANS 10:12,17 THE MESSAGE)

Soon after I married, I (Sharon) began attending a Bible study with a group of terrific ladies. The study was good, the people were pleasant, the food was wonderful, and I ... well, I was perfectly miserable. Each week I would drag myself through the door of our home, telling my husband how awful I was compared to the other ladies. "Her hair is so cute! I want to get my hair cut," I'd pout. "And she always has her fingernails done! She has the cutest clothes! She made the best food! I feel like I never cook anymore!" With disgust I would say, "You should have seen her house. Well, I'm glad you didn't, because you'd be ashamed of our house if you saw hers. She always says just the right things, and my words are always wrong."

I also felt like I didn't come close to the godly character found in the sweet ladies at Bible study. I didn't have children at the time, but becoming a mom has given me even more ammunition for my comparisons: "She is such a better mom than me. Did you see her wipe the entire shopping cart with a wet wipe before she put her child in it? Why don't I ever think of things like that? She even stuck a plastic bag in her diaper bag, just in case the baby's clothes got wet. She's amazing. I'm terrible! Her kids mind her so much better than my kids mind me. What's wrong with me?" Constantly comparing . . . that was (and sometimes still is) me.

After weeks of hearing me compare myself to the women at Bible study, my sweet husband looked at me and said, "Honey, I don't think you need to go back there anymore. I don't think it's good for you."

a wake-up call

Like being dowsed with cold water, my husband's statement made me suddenly aware of my self-centered focus. I realized I had robbed myself of the joy of fellowship with precious women, the joy of studying God's Word, and the joy of realizing God made me for a specific and unique purpose. When joy is missing, misery comes calling, and I was miserable. I was discontented with who I was, the person God had made me to be. I was too busy trying to be like everybody else, envious of their appearance, their ability to communicate, their expertise in cooking and cleaning—and now, with children—their mothering skills, to notice how God had equipped me.

Julie Barnhill writes:

> In all likelihood, our mothers never handed us an instruction guide entitled "How to Live a Miserable, Comparing Lifestyle." . . . Yet every day, everywhere, from every age bracket, and even despite our faith in Jesus Christ, we size each other up, comparing supposed weaknesses and trying to make ourselves feel better by ignoring or brushing off one another. . . . Simply put, when my thoughts are filled with worrying about those I perceive as better or "other" than me, I change the way I relate to others. I cut off the very supply chain of female friendships I was created to enjoy.[1]

My comparing routine made my life lonely, void of close friends, out of order, and seemingly useless. All I could see was that I couldn't do anything right. "Where you have envy and selfish ambition, there you find disorder" (James 3:16). The closets and drawers of my mind were cluttered with every inadequacy imaginable. I felt I would never measure up! As moms, don't we all feel that way at times?

"Don't be envious of the runner in the lane next to you; just focus on finishing *your* race," states Rick Warren.[2] Your value is not dependent on how you stack up next to someone else. You are not your sister, your mother, your friend, your neighbor, or anyone else you think or wish you should resemble. "As you learn more and more how God works, you will learn how to do *your* work" (Colossians 1:10 THE MESSAGE, emphasis added).

By looking at others as our standard for how we should look, how we should speak to our children, and how we should respond to life, we are actually telling God by our actions and attitude that we *disapprove* of how *He* made us. Like a selfish teenager we fuss and argue with Him about our differences rather than enjoying our uniqueness.

getting your focus right

Have you ever held a camera at arm's length and snapped a picture of yourself? The results (unless your arms are longer than mine) are fuzzy and anything but attractive. As a mom I find my mind's camera often points back at me rather than looking outward through the lens at how things really are. When I zoom in on *me,* I suddenly notice all my inadequacies, distorted, of course, by the odd angle of the camera.

To take a "good" picture, we need to turn the camera around so we're able to focus on someone else. When our camera is pointed at "yours truly," we miss everyone else. We miss out on what we could give to others and what we could learn from them. How do we stop doing this? We must ask the Lord on a regular basis to nudge us when we start comparing ourselves with others and despising how He's made us. Then we need to ask Him to help us turn our cameras around and stop focusing on ourselves. Where *should* our focus be?

focus on God first

Jesus said that the greatest commandment is " 'Love the Lord your God with all your heart and with all your soul and with all your mind and with all your strength'" (Mark 12:30). You might be thinking, *What does that have to do with my comparing myself to other people?* It has everything to do with it, because rather than focusing on yourself, you zoom your camera in as far as possible on the living God. The God that made you has so much insight, love, and hope that He wants to share with you. When you focus on Him rather than yourself you'll find joy.

So turn your camera around and focus on how you can love God. Talk to Him throughout your day, listen to praise music, and let your kids help you learn some key Bible verses that will transform your attitude. Even though time is limited for moms, make it a high priority (especially when you find yourself discontented with who you are) to spend time reading His Word and praying for yourself and your family.

My friend Marylyn told me, "For moms, it's usually not a 'quiet' time. The kids don't have to be asleep for you to spend time with God. Sometimes it's 'loud' time, but no less precious when it's time spent with the Father." It doesn't have to be an hour either. Fifteen minutes devoted to getting to know God can change the outcome of your whole day.

A single mom shared her ways of keeping her focus on God: "Get involved in women's groups at church, women's Bible studies, women's conferences, daily Bible study with God, but most importantly, keep Bible verses in front of you constantly (in your car-drive time, at your desk at work, at home), and worship (I sing in the car and during the day)—that keeps your focus above" (Karen).

focus on others

The first commandment is to love the Lord your God with all your heart, soul, mind, and strength. But Jesus went on to say in Mark 12:31, "The second [commandment] is this: 'Love your neighbor as yourself.'"

Notice the order of those commandments: Love God first, then love your neighbor. If we try to love our neighbor first it won't work. God knew that would result in our comparing ourselves to other moms and being discontented with who we are.

As women it's hard for us to accept ourselves, much less think that God could love and accept us just the way we are. Therefore we do "good" things in an attempt to earn God's approval. But make sure you get this: God's love for you is *not* dependent on what *you* do. You cannot earn His love. He just loves you. *He loves you.* You can't change that.

Our doing for others can't add one more ounce to the love God already has for us. It's not like a scale we are trying to balance, with God's love on one side and our good deeds on the other. That's not how it works.

When Jesus died for you and me, He tipped the scale of God's love all the way in our favor, then super-glued it down. Nothing can make the scale tilt the other way . . . nothing. We can never do anything to make Him love us more, or less. It should be out of love and respect for our heavenly Father that we give and do for our neighbors.

Because He loves you and me so much, He wants to *help* us love our neighbors as we love ourselves. It's like He loans us His camera to see people. He gives us the strength to love all our neighbors, the ones in our house and those out of our house. "If anyone serves, he should do it with the strength God provides, so that in all things God may be praised through Jesus Christ" (1 Peter 4:11b). Through Him we *can* love others.

It's amazing to me that when my focus is on the Lord and I'm doing what He wants me to do, I am more patient with my family and I don't compare myself to others. I am more willing to listen when my child has had a hard day; I'm happier to see my husband walk through the door; I'm more open to praying with a friend about the loss of her husband's job; I am more available to listen to a mom tell the funny things her children said, and I am able to empathize with the struggles a fellow mom may be having with siblings who fight constantly.

God is able to change my focus and help me genuinely care about the "neighbors" in my life. When my eyes are on the Lord, He gives me the strength to be "quick to listen, slow to speak and slow to become angry" (James 1:19) with my neighbors, even my *closest neighbors*.

Our Closest Neighbors

We often forget that our closest neighbors are those living under our roof. It's easy for me to think of my neighbor as the lady across the street, the mom at my daughter's gymnastics class, or the friend at church who needs support. And it's true that they are all "neighbors," but sometimes the "neighbors" who are most difficult to love are those I live with! What about the guy whose socks I have matched a thousand times? Am I supposed to consider him my neighbor? What about the kids who track mud on my clean floor? I'm supposed to love them as myself? Could "love your neighbor as yourself" apply to my family as well? The answer is YES!

You may be thinking, "Oh no! That's too hard!" But keep reading . . . don't give up now. We will talk more about being content with your husband and children in the following chapters.

three photo albums

As moms we are constantly taking pictures of ourselves and we choose to categorize these images in one of three albums.

In photo album #1 we find snapshots of a woman who is always comparing herself to others—her body, her habits, the financial status of her family, and her skills. She has the overwhelming feeling that she has nothing to offer the world. She is constantly striving to be something or someone she was not meant to be. She feels like she is not capable of doing enough as a mom or friend, and she always worries about what others are thinking of her.

Beneath the cover of photo album #2 we find a smiling woman. But if you look closely, it's not her smile, but one she cut out and pasted to her face (kind of like those hips on magazine covers). She is focused on other people, sort of. With her plastered smile she "listens" to her friend while organizing the rest of the day in her head. She musters her energy to prepare an extra-special meal for her husband, but is frustrated by the end of it because the cake didn't rise. She offers to help with the nursery, only to find herself wishing she hadn't. She goes to bed exhausted from the day, dreading the start of tomorrow. She is tired-out and burned-out. She wonders how she can keep up this pace.

Then last, inside photo album #3, we find another woman. She is the one the first woman longs to be like and the one the second lady works hard to match. She has a listening ear for a friend even when it means the plan for her day will change. She looks at other women with God's loving camera, being more concerned about how someone feels than how they dress. Because she is depending on God's strength, she is able to instruct and train rather than yell at her child. She spends time with God not out of duty but because she loves Him. She climbs into bed at night and thanks God for His goodness.

Does the lady in photo album #3 sound a little too perfect? Don't worry, she's not. It's just that by spending time with God she has learned to be more and more like Him. Her eyes have been focused on the Lord, and He has kept His promise: "Those who look to him are radiant; their faces are never covered with shame" (Psalm 34:5). It isn't something that happened to her overnight.

Actually, she has three photo albums just like you and me. She has been through those same stages. On occasion she still adds photos to those first two albums—comparing, then doing all she can to measure up. But gradually she began walking more in step with the Lord, dealing with spills and schedules more calmly, thinking the best of her family and friends. And as she did, her third photo album began to grow. Because of her focus on the Lord she is able to love *God*; therefore, she is able to love her *neighbors* (friends, co-workers, husband, children); and now she is even able to love *herself*. Wow—three for one! We're moms, and we know a good deal when we see one!

When we choose to see ourselves and others from God's viewpoint there will be joy, regardless of our circumstances. When He is the focus, it takes the pressure off of us. "Fix your attention on God. You'll be changed from the inside out. Readily recognize what he wants from you, and quickly respond to it. Unlike the culture around you, always dragging you down to its level of immaturity, God brings the best out of you, develops well-formed maturity in you" (Romans 12:2 THE MESSAGE).

So there are three focal points to choose from. The choice seems obvious, but there are days I still find myself in album #1, comparing myself to every woman I meet (usually this happens at one particular time of the month). More frequently I find myself putting photos in album #2, thinking I can handle everything on my own. But more and more I am opening album #3 as I learn to depend on Jesus, to love Him with all my heart, soul, mind, and strength. It's great when I choose to zoom in on the love of the Lord and let Him fill me up so that I can share His love with those who mean so much to me.

stop, drop, and restore your soul

What a trap we find ourselves in: comparing, striving to measure up, only to be disappointed again, and rarely finding contentment in who we are. Without the hope found in Christ, the problem would become cancerous—consuming us, our family, and our friends.

Do you remember Mrs. Olsen from the TV show *Little House on the*

Prairie? She was a vivid portrayal of one who was always comparing and never finding contentment with who she was or what she had. In turn, she was a suspicious, conniving, repulsive person to be around. (I watched those shows as a child and didn't like Mrs. Olsen then. But now, as a mom, oh my ... she's worse than she was when I was a kid!) Her first two photo albums must have been bursting at the seams; I'm afraid Mrs. Olsen knew little about the third album.

1. Why do you think women compare themselves to others so often?
2. When do you struggle the most with comparing yourself to others?
3. How do you feel when your camera is focused on you?
4. If your life—your words, actions, and attitudes—could be made into scrapbooks, which album would have the most pages? Would there be lots of pictures and stories in your "constantly comparing" album? How full would your "trying to handle it all" album be? How often do you add to that third album, the one that finds you leaning on the Lord for strength?
5. How have you seen God change your view of yourself and others as a result of first focusing on Him?

Father,

You know our tendency as women to be unhappy with who we are. Nudge me, Lord, when even a hint of comparison begins to come my way so that I can refocus my attention on You. Help me make time to get to know You. Show me how You created me uniquely to love You with all my heart, soul, mind, and strength. I want to handle things like You would a little more every day. I pray You'll encourage me by letting me see changes that You have made in my life. Thank you, Lord, for your forgiveness and for always being there to help me refocus.

Bless others through me. I pray in Jesus' name. Amen.

making the most of the moments

1. **fuzzy face!** Take an arm's-length picture of yourself. Have it developed and pin it up somewhere to remind you to focus

on God rather than yourself.

2. **unending love** Cut out several hearts and write the following verse on them: "And I pray that you, being rooted and established in love, may have power ... to grasp how wide and long and high and deep is the love of Christ" (Ephesians 3:17b–18). Tape them up in front of your kitchen sink (and other places) so you can read its message when you have a minute.

chapter eight

we've been mediatized!
How the Media Affects Contentment in Women

---

*After watching a popular show for several weeks,
I caught myself treating my husband like he was an idiot!
Suddenly he wasn't as smart as he had always been,
and I was less likely to overlook things that
normally wouldn't have bothered me.*

Sharon

**I'm doing the very best I can, and I'm doing it at home,
where it counts. I refuse to take a second look
at corrupting people and degrading things.**

(PSALM 101:3 THE MESSAGE)

have you been mediatized? Our level of contentment as women can be greatly affected by what we allow to influence us. And many times we don't even realize it is happening. The media plays a significant role in shaping our view of ourselves.

I (Sharon) stood there in the checkout line at the grocery store with magazines to entertain me and candy to occupy my daughter. But today Brittlea was drawn to a magazine at her eye level, right above the sweet stuff. The lady on the cover was wearing a dress with a v neck, and I mean a capital "V." In fact, it was so "V" cut that the tip of the V ended below her belly button! My daughter said, "Mommy, look at that girl on that magazine." I asked her, "What do you notice about the girl on the cover?" A bit embarrassed, she replied, "She's showin' her ta-ta's!" (That's our undercover word for breasts.)

As I glanced at another magazine I noticed it had the same girl on it, but this time she was in a modest, beautiful blouse that highlighted her face. I pointed to that cover and asked, "What do you notice about this girl?" Brittlea replied, "I notice her face. She is so pretty, Mommy." I had her look back at the face of the girl she had noticed on the first cover. She realized it was the same girl and the point was made. Because of her clothing (or lack thereof), she hadn't noticed the face of the girl on the v-neck picture. I was thankful for the opportunity to encourage her to dress so that people will notice her face rather than be distracted by her body.

But it made me think about all the media messages we as women are bombarded with from the time we are little girls. Those subtle hints that whisper what we should look like and how we should act, the instructions for the *right way* to do everything (and I do mean everything)—these all slowly shape our opinion of what is "normal." Unless we talk about it, it is easy to mindlessly follow these messages that are played out in front of us.

I was reminded that I need to not only tell my daughter what is real and normal for her but also make sure I'm certain of what is real and normal for me as a mom. If I don't think about what I'm seeing in magazines, on television, or at the movies, my thoughts will be shaped by my society rather than by God's standards. The psalmist wrote, "Turn my eyes away from worthless things" (Psalm 119:37).

Believing the lies of the media will be sure to produce discontentment. Sometimes we need to be reminded about what is real, and usually what we hear from television, movies, and magazines doesn't go in that category! So let's walk through the media available to us and see what changes we might need to make to help us overcome discontentment.

media messages

As moms we are usually careful about what our kids see because we know it affects their behavior and can fill them with unnecessary fears. But it's easy to become complacent about what *our own eyes* see. What we view affects our behavior, attitudes, and thoughts too. It doesn't take long for television programs to put unrealistic expectations in our heads.

We've grown so accustomed to what the media throws at us that we are rarely bothered by it anymore. Dr. Robert Kubey pinpointed the primary messages of the media as: "(1) materialism; (2) for everything there is a quick fix; (3) young is better; (4) open and unfilled time is not desirable—in fact, it cannot be tolerated; (5) religion is unacceptable; and (6) sex is only good outside of marriage."[1]

Even commercials have a mission. "Advertising executives set out to convince us that we have to have it all—that it's not fair for other people to have more stuff than we do."[2] If we know that those are the messages the media wants us to believe, it makes sense that we would think about how much time we are going to give to it. The old cliché "Garbage in, garbage out" applies to all of us, even moms.

soap opera sagas

While writing this book, I (Sharon) spent several afternoons in a local hotel lobby. The quiet atmosphere and soft music seemed to soothe the words out of me. But sometimes, I have to confess, I become distracted by watching people. One particular afternoon I was diligently writing when I noticed a mom with her two children coming in to watch some television. I assumed she was going to find PBS, Nickelodeon, or Disney for the kids on the TV behind me.

After about ten minutes I realized I hadn't heard *Barney, Rolie Polie Olie,* or *Dora the Explorer,* and I noticed that her children weren't even occupied with the TV. Rather, they were just wandering around. *Where's their mom?* I wondered. Turning very inconspicuously to look, I found her mesmerized by a favorite soap opera, seemingly oblivious to the whereabouts of her kids.

Soap operas can be a trap for moms, especially sleep-deprived new moms. They are addicting, yes, and talk about unrealistic! Who really wakes up looking picture-perfect in the morning? Have you noticed the actresses never have bags under their eyes from being up half the night with a sick child? And can you imagine seeing a woman with "bedhead" on a soap opera? They should put a disclaimer at the beginning of the show: "Nothing in this show is real. But the contents of this show can and will be harmful to the mental and emotional health of all who watch it."

The guys on daytime television are either unbelievably romantic, leading us to think our husbands don't care for us the way they should, or they are jerks, which can make us think *all guys* are just like them! Children are rarely seen on soap operas. Even when they do appear briefly, have you ever heard them after they exit the room? It's as if they've gone to their rooms to play quietly so the mom and dad (maybe he's the dad . . . who knows?) can talk. That's not real life!

If we aren't careful about what we watch, the things we watch become what we *expect*. Then when what we expect isn't what happens in real life, we become discontented. "What boggles the mind is that neither movie nor television characters are ever shown to reap the consequences of their actions. The heroine rarely gets pregnant."[3] And as we all know, real life has consequences.

television traps

We might think of some sitcoms and movies as just good clean fun, but even comedies can give us negative feelings toward our husbands and make us see our children as time-consuming burdens. After watching a popular show for several weeks, I caught myself treating my husband like he was an idiot. Suddenly he wasn't as smart as he had always been, and I was less likely to overlook things that normally wouldn't have bothered me. I decided watching the show wasn't having a positive effect on my attitude toward our marriage, so—as much as I enjoyed that thirty-minute show—I made the choice to stop watching it. I figure I'm critical enough on my own without getting suggestions from Hollywood!

The recent craze to hit American media is known as "reality TV." The shows are sometimes interesting; I've been hooked by more than one of them. I had a hard time sleeping one night worrying that the "bachelor" would choose the self-absorbed snob rather than the sweet girl. Am I the only one who thinks about those shows after the fact? When I'm caught up in a show, I'm busy living someone else's life rather than enjoying my own.

Jeremiah 6:15 says, "They have no shame at all; they do not even know how to blush." Isn't that true of many reality TV stars? I think sometimes they forget that the cameras are on them and the world will soon be watching! Before we get hooked viewing the whole season of a show, we should ask ourselves some hard questions about its content and tone.

Taprina Milburn said in her article, "Examine what you fill your mind with. Does your mental diet consist of tell-all books, despondent music, or television programs that portray the most sinister side of human behavior?"[4] When sinister, degrading behavior is what fills our minds, we can begin to expect that conduct from the people in our lives, and we are capable of changing into that kind of person as well.

Sometimes at night we (my husband and I) find ourselves gravitating to the TV. Sure, I start out with good intentions. I plan to fold the clothes in the overflowing laundry basket while I watch a show. But two hours later I still haven't finished matching the socks, and I am suddenly overwhelmed by all that needs to be done to get ready for the next day.

The next day I'm tired because I was caught up in my favorite decorating show the night before. The crazy thing is, I have heard myself complain about not having enough time to get it all done—after I have essentially wasted two hours in front of the TV. I need to be honest with myself. It's not a problem of not having enough time but my inability to manage my time properly. Television can be more than a time robber— it can negatively affect the whole family.

movie madness

Sharon and I thought our mom and dad were "old fogies" when it came to movies. They wouldn't let us see PG movies until we were at least thirteen (and I think it was more like sixteen). There was no such thing as PG–13 ratings back then, but we wouldn't have been allowed to go to them. R-rated movies were completely out of the question—and they still are for us. What seemed extreme at the time has become a standard we live by.

As a teen I came to my parents with the familiar refrain, "But everybody's doing it!" My dad didn't have much trouble telling me, "*Everybody isn't*, because you're not!" He would go on to explain that what I put into my mind could never be taken out. The good thing about our parents was they wouldn't tell us we couldn't watch something and then watch it themselves. They were diligent at guarding our minds while being protective of their minds as well.

Every weekend a new list of movies appears on the flashing theater billboards across the country. Most of the releases are targeted at teens. As parents we have a big job, often a controversial task, as we try to protect the minds of our kids. Jim Burns, president of Youth-Builders.com, said, "The truth is, we are still in the 'protection business,' even when our kids are teenagers. It's tempting to loosen up a bit when our kids get older because they don't seem so vulnerable. But it is during the teen years that our children are the most susceptible to the siren call of the youth culture created by the entertainment industry." He goes on to say, "Examine your own viewing and listening behavior. When it comes to media, more is caught than taught."[5]

We have to make the decision—one that is unpopular in our society—to shield our minds from sex, violence, and language that will do nothing to help us be better marriage partners or parents. In making that choice, we are teaching our children to protect their minds as well. One mom said, "I want to be a better person since I have become a mom. The choices I make and the way I spend my time are so much more important now. If I am a lazy couch potato, then my child will be too. If I think reading is fun, he does too." (Jill)

Did you grow up in a home that didn't pay much attention to movie content? If so, you might not have considered the impact movies have had or can have on your level of contentment. If you find yourself in a theater feeling uncomfortable with what is happening on the big screen, it is fine to get up and walk out. Take heart and be diligent about your movie choices. Before you go to a movie and blow your bucks on a less than great flick, check it out. A Christian movie review for any movie in the theater can be found at *www.pluggedinonline.org* (click on movies). Other helpful resources are:

> **Clean Films** (*www.cleanfilms.com*)—a company that takes inappropriate content out of movies. There is a small fee (far less than you'd pay at the theater) to have cleaned-up popular movies sent to your mailbox.
>
> **TV Guardian** (*www.tvguardian.com*)—This technology works with the closed captioning of programs in order to mute the sound. It has three levels of strictness for you to choose from. TVguardian.com will give you information about their products and where to find them.

magazines—another form of media

Just like other forms of media, magazines have a way of shaping our expectations of what "real" should be for us. Today there are rows and rows of beauty and home magazines that line the store shelves. When I look at those "perfect" photos, I subconsciously decide that I should look like the girls on the magazine covers and that my house should look just as perfect as the cover photo. There are several problems with both of those crazy expectations:

1. *Sometimes their "beauty" makes me feel like the "beast"!*

   Reasons we won't ever look like the girls on the magazine cover:

   • Airbrushed images look *better* than the real thing. We don't have access to airbrush, but at least people know they're getting the real thing when they look at us. My hips belong to me and aren't some computer-generated hips from somebody with a more appealing figure.

   • Children—We carried them for nine months, then birthed them. (Even if you adopted your children, somehow we all get that "mommy shape.") We probably won't ever have (probably never did have, even before babies) the kind of body the models possess. But don't despair—they are probably too skinny anyway.

   • Clothes—I could never afford the clothes they model, and quite frankly, I (proudly) wear more than they do!

2. *Home isn't a magazine cover; it's where we live!*

   Why don't we have the "perfectly" decorated haven?

   • We have kids! At no time will our home be perfectly picked up like on the magazine cover.

   • We can't afford it. Houses in magazines have big budgets.

   • We don't have time. (Like we talked about earlier, I don't want to spend all of my time on the house. I'd rather spend it with my family.)

A mom in California told us that she was thrilled when an editor of a home magazine wanted to feature her home in their magazine. Her husband, wise to the idea, asked, "What will this involve from me?" She told him they would be pleased with the house as it was. But *four months* later, when it was time for the photo shoot, her husband was less than happy about having to re-carpet, repaint, and re-everything before the photographers arrived! Knowing that it takes so much time to make a house look just right, how can I expect my house to be picture-perfect? And why would I want to have it that way? My time (and my husband thinks his time too) is better spent on other things.

As little girls, teens, young women, and now moms, we have been fed the lie that it's normal to have a perfect house, perfect husband, perfect figure, perfect children, perfect career, i.e., a perfect life. Many of those messages were passed on to us through the various avenues of the media. In her book *Choices,* Mary Farrar uncovers the myths society has fed us. A stunned college-age girl, after hearing Farrar speak about the deceptive expectations we have developed about life, told Mary:

> "You said, 'No one can have it all.' You said the idea that 'you can have it all' is a lie. I've been told all my life that I can have it all. I've lived my whole life on that philosophy. Everything I've done, every decision I've made has been to that end. And I've worked so hard—just to make it happen!"

Mary concluded, "A good lie wraps itself around just enough truth to draw its listeners in."[6] A lot of good lies are wrapped around media messages. We have been drawn in, moms. It's up to us to accept the truth: *We cannot have it all.* If you find yourself striving to have it all, trying to live up to what the media says is "normal," you're probably miserable, sorely disappointed, and completely discontented with the life God has given you. A thankful heart is rarely a discontented one. If you focus on what you don't have rather than the blessings that are yours, you will be unhappy. But if you make yourself dwell on what you are thankful for, you will find contentment.

God's perspective on the media

Jesus said, " 'The eye is the lamp of the body. If your eyes are good, your whole body will be full of light. But if your eyes are bad, your whole body will be full of darkness. If then the light within you is darkness, how great is that darkness!' " (Matthew 6:22–23). Since our eyes play such an important part in our bodies, it is important for me to be careful with what my eyes see.

The last of the Ten Commandments is "You shall not covet your neighbor's house. You shall not covet your neighbor's wife [husband] . . . or anything that belongs to your neighbor" (Exodus 20:17). God didn't give us boundaries to make us suffer and keep us from having a good time. He knew that when we desire or covet what others have, we will be bound by disappointment and envy. He gave us limits to protect us so we can be free from the effects of discontentment.

It may seem relaxing and freeing to watch whatever we want to watch or to read whatever we want to read. However, if what we put into our minds is going to make us discontented with what we presently have and cause us to mistreat those we love, we aren't really free at all. We are all tied up doing things we don't want to do, instead of being free to do what we really want to do as God's children.

It's like us as parents. We give our kids boundaries, such as "Don't play in the street" to protect them, not to spoil their fun. God loves us as His children even more and wants to lead us through life in such a way that we experience joy and peace. He knows that when we look outside of what we have with longing, we'll feel discontented with what we have.

When we fill our minds with things the world offers, we'll live like the world. Philippians 4:8 gives us courage to go against the grain of society and be intentional about what we allow into our minds. Rather than filling our minds with what the world offers, Paul says, "You'll do best by filling your minds and meditating on things true, noble, reputable, authentic, compelling, gracious—the best, not the worst; the beautiful, not the ugly. . . . God who makes everything work together, will work you into his most excellent harmonies" (Philippians 4:8–9 THE MESSAGE). "Garbage in, garbage out" is a true statement, but so is "Good stuff in, good stuff out"! Put in the good stuff and let Him "work you into His most excellent harmonies."

stop, drop, and restore your soul

Does what you watch breed discontentment with who you are and what you have? Have magazines ever made you feel inadequate (or made your husband look less than adequate)? Subtle invitations into a world of fantasy can lead us into the desert of discontentment. We have a choice— not always an easy one—to watch or not to watch, to compare or not to compare. Have you been mediatized?

1. How many hours do you watch reality shows, soap operas,

regular TV shows, or movies each week?

2. How does what you watch affect how you think, how you treat your family, how much you accomplish, how late you go to bed, and how content you are with your life?

3. Are you selective about the movies you watch? If yes, what is your personal standard? If no, what is a reasonable boundary you could set for yourself?

4. Are there any television habits you feel you would like to change? What are they?

5. Now that you know how long it takes to have a magazine-worthy house and body, how are you going to move toward being content with the home and body God has blessed you with?

Lord,

You have given us incredible minds, minds that remember what we see, so help us to watch the good stuff and not the bad. Help us to think before we thoughtlessly spend time or money on things that won't satisfy in the long run. Help us to evaluate what the media offers and to see it for what it is. In Jesus' name. Amen.

making the most of the moments

1. **tv-free week!** Declare it "TV-Free Week" at your house. Pull out a puzzle and work it *together*, play board games or charades. (For those whiny TV addicts, you could tell them that TV-Free Week won't end until they finish the puzzle. Who knows, they may ask for another puzzle when they're finished with the first one. If not, at least you've had some great time together.)

2. **what's on the media menu?** Make a list of all the media in your life. Try going on a media diet, cutting out two things on your list, and see if you have more time to do the things you really want to do.

3. **filling in the gaps** When you make changes about what you are putting into your mind, try filling those holes with praise and worship music and by putting Scripture quotes around your house to remind you what is true and right.

chapter nine

married . . . and loving it?

Finding Real Contentment in Marriage

---

*To get the full value of a joy you must
have somebody to divide it with.*
Mark Twain

**Two are better than one, because they have a
good return for their work.**

(ECCLESIASTES 4:9)

my husband and I (Sharon) stood in the hallway, three kids pulling on us as we made our way to each of their separate classrooms at church. We hadn't just had the common fight on the way to church (getting us in a worshipful mood). No, we had been at odds all week.

My husband could do nothing right it seemed! I decided he was not only oblivious to my world but also to the world around him. Like a magnet to a refrigerator, so was my husband to his laptop; I was angry that he spent so much time on it, ignoring the fact that his office was a mess. He fussed at the kids too much (I'm the monitor of that, you know). Then I noticed his careless driving habits, that he hadn't put his clothes away—again, and he snacked right after we had just eaten a meal. What kind of example is that? As you can see, I'm such a *wonderful* example to our children—of how to judge people!

As we were dragging our offspring through the halls that Sunday morning, suddenly it was as if the world moved in slow motion. I saw him—this man, about my husband's age, looking at his wife, who was holding their toddler. He tilted his head lovingly and said, "I love you, sweetie. I'll see you after the service." She responded with a loving, respectful I-can't-wait-to-see-you smile and the words, "Bye, sweet." I was standing in the middle of the hall, staring, mouth dropped open, unable to move, until my children yanked me back to reality. At that point I wanted to join the babies in the nursery nearby. They were crying, and I could have wailed with the best of them.

Feelings of failure and guilt, and questions about my devotion as a wife, flooded my mind during that eight-second episode of love played out in front of me. "She was so loving to her husband. I can't believe she looked at him so starry-eyed! Do I ever look at my husband that way?" As we trudged on to the children's classes, I felt as if someone had thrown a fifty-pound weight around my neck.

In that short encounter I had figured out my version of the couple's life story. I decided that she was a wife who never suffered from PMS (which I realized I was facing head-on), a woman who encouraged her husband in his role as a dad, and someone who noticed all the things that he did to help around the house. I, on the other hand, had missed all the things my husband had done that week—washed loads and loads of laundry, emptied the dishwasher, read books to the kids, and provided for our family while on that time-taking laptop.

Sometimes it's easy to focus on the negative things. And when we stay there too long, it's hard to see how our deteriorating relationship could ever get any better. Remembering why we married him gets lost in the sea of disappointments and failures. But don't give up. Hold on.

no advance training

In marriage, just as in parenting, you get no real training before you're full-time into the relationship. How are you supposed to know how to be married? TV (as we discussed earlier) has lots of suggestions . . . mostly scary ones! Your parents gave you a picture of marriage, but maybe they divorced and shook your view of a forever relationship. Even if you were raised in a two-parent home, it's possible that they weren't the best example of a loving relationship—maybe they just stayed together "for the kids." Or maybe your parents were terrific. But just because they openly showed their love for each other and they knew how to be married doesn't mean you automatically know how to do this marriage thing. You're a different person than your parents, which means you won't do things exactly like them. And your husband is different as well. Just as every lock has a unique key to make it work, each union between a man and a woman is going to work in its own unique way.

the "d" word

During an argument early in our marriage (over how to wash clothes), my exasperated husband made the comment, "What are you going to do, divorce me?" I was shocked, but mostly hurt by his words. How could the "D" word come up at all, especially when we were just fussing about a load of laundry? I fell on our bed and burst into tears. We both apologized, but what we did next was priceless. We made a commitment that we would never even bring up the "D" word again. In that commitment I find security. I don't worry about his seeking a divorce and I don't hold divorce over his head as a threat to get him to shape up. We simply took it out of our vocabulary.

Lin, a wife of thirty years, wrote:

> I wish someone had told me that the first time you fall out of love—the marriage is not over. I remember crying and crying the first time I didn't "feel" love for my husband (and I adore him). The truth is that feelings come and go, only to return again. The important thing is the commitment to the Lord and to each other. I'm in the season of life where this is my second marriage—it's just the same husband. It's much sweeter for having gone through those difficult times. Be encouraged—don't give up.

Marriage is hard and at times unfair, and it doesn't always feel good, but that's just how it is. During our marriage I've had the thought on several occasions, *How can I live with him for the rest of my life?* (I'm sure my husband has had the same thoughts about me.) But because of my commitment to stick it out until death, it's not an issue of *how to get out* but rather *how to stay in!*

a large and monumental task

Why is marriage so hard? I knew there would be struggles, but this is so much work, and now that I'm a mom, I'm really tired! I was relieved to find compassion in Jesus' teaching in Matthew 19. He says,

"'Not everyone is mature enough to live a married life. It requires a certain aptitude and grace. Marriage isn't for everyone. . . . But if you're capable of growing into the largeness of marriage, do it'" (vv. 11–12 THE MESSAGE). I'm convinced that if we are married, we are capable of growing into the largeness of marriage with God's strength. But it is a huge undertaking, something we must grow into. Marriage is a relationship we start learning about the day we get married, and if we're smart we'll keep learning for the rest of our lives.

It's encouraging to know that marriage is no picnic for anyone. Marriage is work for every couple, no matter how easy they make it look. Research shows that the couples that have good marriages have the same amount of conflict that people with troubled marriages have. The difference is in how they deal with it. Marriage is worth the work. Don't give in just because it gets hard.

It's good to have some tips up your sleeve for those times when you feel hopeless and when criticism is on the tip of your tongue. Here are some of our favorites:

tip 1: let your face be his refuge

I've walked by the mirror at times and caught a glimpse of myself. To my surprise, I looked horrible! It wasn't simply that my hair and makeup weren't fixed, or that I was still in my pajamas, but I just looked angry. I wasn't particularly upset about anything, but my face looked as though I'd just taken a sip of those sour apple juice bags my kids love to drink. I realized that I needed to smile more. Smiling makes you feel better. And guess who else feels better when Mom smiles? Husbands and kids really appreciate a smile from the main lady in the house.

Unfortunately, the saying is true: "If Momma ain't happy, ain't nobody happy." I long for my face to be my family's refuge. The world can be a cruel place for our husbands and children. If they come home to a disagreeable, discontented wife/mom, their place of safety becomes uncomfortable for them. Some synonyms of refuge describe what a cheerful look can be for our family: a safe haven, a sanctuary, a shelter, a place of safety and protection, a harbor, and a retreat. It is my goal for my husband to look at me, no matter where we are, and feel "safe." The neat thing is, when my face is loving, loving words and actions usually follow.

This is my *goal*—not something I've completely achieved, but what I'm aiming for. I have to remind myself that this is my goal or I fall into a marital slump and my face slides back into the sour-apple pose again. The couple I saw at church reminded me that I was doing it again—looking disagreeable. By the look on her husband's face, I knew he had found a safe place in her face—at least that day. She's probably not that way all the time either. But that incident jolted me out of my selfish, discouraging frame of mind and back into the reality I want to live in, one of love and encouragement for my husband.

tip 2: things aren't always as they seem

I might be seeing only the negative things, but by reminding myself that things aren't always as they seem, I can realize that my perceptions might be "crooked" at this point in time. If my husband seems extra irritable with the kids, remembering that "things aren't always as they seem" can help me look at him with understanding rather than judgment. Is something bothering him about work, is he worried about money, is he wishing he exercised more, is there something between us that needs to be cleared up? Like kicking the cat at the end of a bad day, maybe his frustration is prompted by something else, not just the kids.

Here's another example of how to use this tip: If you have a preschooler, your husband could think you're just not interested in him anymore because sex isn't as high on your list of priorities as it once was. You might question your lack of sexual feelings too. But remember, sleep deprivation and exhaustion can cause that lack of interest in intimacy for a time. Not that you need to excuse yourself from all "extracurricular activities," but this is another area where "things aren't as they seem" at this moment. It won't always be this way; you will be interested again. Let your hubby know that you love him, and assure him that you won't always be this exhausted.

Once I (Laurie) was in the car with my husband, Charles, who was being noticeably quiet—more than usual. I started thinking, *I wonder what's wrong? Did I say something that made him mad? Oh, it must have been that I didn't pick up the batteries he asked me to buy for the camera. I'm so forgetful. I can't remember anything lately. No wonder he's mad at me!* And with that I blurted through the silence, "Honey, I'm sorry I'm so forgetful. I know you're upset. I really want to work on that."

"That's okay," he replied, seemingly unconcerned. Then there was silence again. I decided by his apathetic response that something must still be bothering him. "Sweetie, what's wrong?"

He looked at me, puzzled, and said, "Nothing."

"Well, why are you being so quiet? What are you thinking about?" I asked.

"I was thinking about how I could fix the problem I'm having with my computer."

Men and women. We are so different, aren't we? As women we have a tendency to overanalyze our relationships. Sometimes we should just wait and not scrutinize every comment, every grunt, every groan, every moan, or every sigh. This tip can help us remember not to get angry when the whole situation isn't yet clear. It can also help us to assume the best instead of the worst. Proverbs 15:18 says, "A hot-tempered [wife] stirs up dissension, but a patient [wife] calms a quarrel."

tip 3: admit you're struggling before you burst!

Have you ever blown up a balloon bigger and bigger, thinking with every breath it was going to burst? Finally it does. Before it popped, you had two choices: to keep blowing until it popped, or to stop and let the air out. When we become angry, disgruntled, or get in a funk for whatever reason, we have two choices: to let the anger rise until we burst with angry words, or admit we are struggling and end the pressure buildup. That sounds so easy, but it's hard to do when you feel justified in your anger.

I've noticed that if I go on without telling my husband I'm struggling, I eventually blow up at him. But if I swallow my pride, admit I'm wrong, and just tell him I'm struggling, it "lets the air out," breaks down the wall I've been building, stops the vicious cycle, and as a result we can peacefully move on. My husband can be so understanding and loving when he knows I'm having a tough day. That's so much better than saying things that are hurtful to him, words I'll later regret.

tip 4: goals vs. desires

Often it's easy for us to want our husbands to change, when *we* might be the real problem. One mom said, "My greatest struggle as a wife is having too many expectations! I expect so much from my husband that

I often take him for granted. . . . I need to work on appreciating him more and expecting nothing." Great idea . . . but how do we do it?

When we were newly married, we (Pat and Sharon) heard a cassette of Jack and Cynthia Heald explaining Larry Crabb's definition of "goals" and "desires" in marriage. It made so much sense to us. I think the answer to appreciating rather than expecting is found there. A goal is something I can set for myself. If I want to read my Bible every day, that's a goal, because I can control that. If I want to exercise every day, that's a goal. Maybe I want to make it my goal to cook more. Those are all things I can control.

On the other hand, a desire is anything that I want that involves another person. Say I want my husband to play with the kids more, or be more affectionate with me, or maybe I want him to drive more carefully. Those are desires, because I can't control how he lives his life. The trouble comes when we try to make our desires into our goals. When that happens, we end up nagging our husbands. You know what that accomplishes, right? Nothing! It actually pushes them further from what we want. So with goals, those things you can control, work hard at them. But with desires, those things that aren't all up to you, *pray*.

My "image" of a perfect Christian husband included this small dream: Each night he would gently take me by the hand, invite me to kneel beside him, and we would have an amazing prayer life together! Well, it didn't work out like that. . . . in fact, when we were first married, we never prayed together. After a time, I realized how much I longed for Mark to step up and really be the leader in our relationship in all ways—not just praying FOR me, but praying WITH me. I was afraid to mention it to him because I thought it would put pressure on him, and I felt like it should be something he felt led to do . . . so I prayed and prayed that God would touch Mark in such a way that he would feel compelled to lead the two of us in prayer . . . and then . . . he took my hand, led me to our bedroom, and knelt by my side to lead us in amazing prayer. All I could do was just cry. It was such an answered prayer! God brought the "leader" out in my husband, and I didn't have to mention it, beg for it, or cajole him into it! It doesn't happen every night, and we both want it to happen more—but that is a growing thing for us, and we are loving watching God at work. (Kelly)

The great thing about praying is that it takes the pressure off of you. The manipulating ends. God is free to change your husband if that's what needs to happen, but He is also free to change you. I daresay that most of the time it isn't my husband who needs changing—it's me! So pray, pray, pray and see what God can do.

tip 5: think, *i love you.*

Some of you may be reading this and thinking, "Yeah, but you don't know *my* husband." You're right. And there are marriages plagued by resentment, unfaithfulness, spousal abuse, financial difficulties, pornography, and alcohol or drug abuse. My heart breaks for those of you in tough situations. I know there are marriages that some of you didn't choose to leave, but instead he left you. And for those of you in abusive situations and those who have suffered through unfaithfulness over and over, I know the marriage might not be mendable.

But for many marriages, women bail out at the first sign of trouble and never get to see what God could do in their tough circumstances. Kathy Collard Miller, a wife and mom of two, openly shared about her troubled marriage in their early years. Her husband was rarely home; he never helped with the two children or spent time with them; he didn't understand how deeply she was struggling; and he didn't seem to care how she was feeling. One day before he came home, she had the thought, *Tell him you love him when he walks through the door.* She was astonished at this irrational idea. She could hardly talk to the man, much less tell him she loved him. So she brushed the thought aside and went on about her business. When the thought came along again, she said, "God, I will not tell him that I love him." And she again went on with her day. Then she had the thought, *Well, just look at him and think it.* She reluctantly said, "Okay, maybe that's not too threatening, God. I can do that."

When her husband walked through the door that day she said it was hard—like squeezing juice from a used lemon—but she formed the thought into her mind. Nothing changed immediately. She still didn't like him, but she did it again the next day, and the next, until finally she was able to *speak* the words to him. In time God changed both of them and restored their marriage. Kathy's obedience and willingness not to give up on what looked like a hopeless marriage softened her heart, and eventually her actions and feelings matched her words: "I love you."

If you are at a point in your marriage where you feel there is no hope, a place you never thought you'd be, look up. You don't know what the rewards of staying together in the hard times might hold for you, your husband, and your children. Our dad says, "The grass always looks greener on the other side of the fence, but that grass has to be mowed too!" The world says, "Oh, go ahead—leave him. You deserve better; he doesn't do anything for you; you'd be better off without him. There's something better right around the corner." But our God says, don't be afraid to grow into this large, sometimes frustrating but priceless relationship called marriage. If you have to start with just thinking, *I love you,* start there.

i need help!

It's important to get training for marriage. Sometimes we need the help that others can give us to make ours work better. Though you can't make your husband seek help, you can find avenues of training for yourself. Here are some ideas:

1. *Godly Friends.* Talking to a friend about your struggles in marriage can be great *if* she doesn't just focus on the negative things about your husband. It's easy for wives to have a "husband bashing" session while sharing all their marital war stories. Every woman needs a girl friend to whom she can vent, but that friend needs to be someone who is not only compassionate but also sees the situation objectively. Taking sides isn't helpful.

2. *Godly Couple Friends.* We know a couple who has a great marriage, and I learn something every time I'm with them. Not that they don't have struggles, but when we go home after spending time with them I see my husband more positively than before. If you don't know anyone like that, pray that God would send such a couple into your lives. Not that you have to have *both* a godly couple and a compassionate/objective girl friend. One of the two is a great gift. Having both is just an added blessing!

3. *Books.* I've noticed that reading books (like this one) is a great resource for growing in marriage. I know that as a mom, it's hard to make time to read, but there are some great books that can really help you along the marriage journey.

4. *Radio Broadcasts*—The radio is a truly "mom-friendly" resource. It offers not only music that can calm your household but also Christian talk shows that can give you so much practical, apply-right-now advice. If you're not familiar with Christian programming, here are some of our favorite programs that offer encouragement on marriage and parenting:

Focus on the Family, *www.family.org,* 1–800-A-Family
Family Life Today, *www.fltoday.org,* 1–800-FL-Today
Living on the Edge Ministries with Chip Ingram, *www.lote.org*
MOMSense Radio with Elisa Morgan, *www.mops.org*
American Family Radio, *www.afr.net*

(Check their Web sites for a radio station and broadcast times in your area.)

stop, drop, and restore your soul

Nobody has it all together in marriage. But sometimes we feel like we are less together in our relationship than everybody else. Marriage is something we grow into. Be patient with yourself and your husband. Don't throw it all away because it's a challenge. That's just part of it. Hang in there. Things aren't always as they seem.

1. What attracted you to your husband when you were dating? How often do you "think about such things" (Philippians 4:8)?
2. Out of the five "tips" that we covered in this chapter, which one was most applicable to you? Which ones would you like God to help you with?
3. What changes can you make immediately that will help you grow in love and contentment with your husband?
4. How much time do you spend with a godly friend or couple?
5. What traits did you initially find attractive in your mate, which now have become frustrating to you? How can you change your perspective about them?

Father,

You know my heart for my husband. You know when I'm glad to be married to him and You know when I'm not so happy about being committed to him. With the demands of children and life sometimes I forget him, Lord. I forget why I was so giggly about him and what we did before we were married. Help me to remember. Restore what we have lost and grow us beyond what we can imagine. Forgive me for missing opportunities to encourage him and for the times when I chose to tear him down instead. Help me to work on myself rather than always trying to "fix" him. I want to love being his wife, just as I want to love being a mom. Help me to persevere when times are tough. Please help us both to grow into the couple You want us to be. Trusting You as I begin again, I pray in Jesus' name. Amen.

making the most of the moments

1. **put your "hand" on my shoulder** One night my husband, Pat, fell asleep with his hand resting on my shoulder. I kissed his hand, then just looked at it. I was suddenly flooded with thoughts about all the things his hands have done—as a baby, as a young man, and as my husband. I remembered the times he massaged my back, held our babies, wiped little bottoms or bandaged owies, pulled baby teeth (with needle-nose pliers), or held tiny fingers as they clung to his. Sometimes it helps us grow in love with our husbands when we stop and think about all they do that is good.

    Get your husband to let you trace his hand. (You could have a family hand-tracing time ... your kids would love it!) After you've outlined his hand, write all the things he has done with those hands and hang it somewhere to remind you to think of him in a loving way during your day.

2. **turn on the radio** Find a Christian radio station that has uplifting music and programs on marriage and family. Turn it on and leave it there. As we listen to positive programming in our homes it not only encourages us, but trains our children as well.

chapter **ten**

we're on the same team ... right?

How Kids Affect Marriage

I think children have enhanced our marriage and at the same time devoured it!
MaryAnn

If you keep on biting and devouring each other, watch out or you will be destroyed by each other.

(Galatians 5:15)

Someone once advised me, "Sharon, your hardest year of marriage will be the first year." So I braced myself for the turbulent ride. Sure we had our differences, but for the most part we enjoyed the 365 days following our wedding. We commemorated all the firsts ... the first Christmas, first Valentine's Day, first anniversary of our first kiss, first furniture we purchased together, first anniversary of our engagement, first family vacation, even our first fight! Pleasantly surprised with how wonderful our first year had been, my husband and I ended that year with an anniversary trip. I cried about it being the close of "the firsts." (Is this nauseating you?) If my informant was correct and this truly was to be the hardest phase of our marriage, I couldn't imagine the bliss awaiting us in the years ahead. But I wasn't thinking about the other "first" that was soon to arrive!

A couple of years later we had a major *first* ... our daughter. Suddenly my husband became so selfish—he didn't seem concerned about my needs, and he was oblivious to all the work that needed to be done. "How can he come home, sit down in the chair, and watch TV, when I so desperately need his help? I never just 'sit down,' at least not while the baby is awake!" We found ourselves fussing over whose turn it was to change the diaper, resenting each other more than the chore.

How had this happened? Was I as uninterested in his life as I felt he was in mine? Over the next months and years, without realizing it, we turned our life together into two separate lives: He worked and I took care of the children.

Laurie had a similar reaction when her children came. She remembers:

> When I was staying home with Alec in those early days, I felt I knew our baby better than my husband and that somehow the baby and I had a bond that was stronger than my marriage bond. After all, this baby was my own flesh and blood. I somehow felt that my child understood and responded to me in a way my husband didn't. A wall began to build, and I felt farther and farther away from him. I began to see myself and my child as "us" (the insiders) and my husband as the outsider. But one day I finally realized that he was still the same man I married, and I had a choice to either work at tearing down the wall between us or continue to build it higher.

We asked lots of moms how children affected their relationship with their husband; here are some of the responses we received:

"Romance, what's that?" (Cindi)

"Having children has definitely added a challenge to our marriage! We appreciate our couple time much more now. We're trying to do things together that we enjoyed while dating." (Amy)

"The intimacy begins to be lacking and you really have to schedule and make time for each other." (Amy C.)

"My husband and I maintain that having children is one of the hardest things a marriage has to endure. Your focus goes from each other to these little people who need everything. However, it's also amazing to see the kids and think that they are a little bit of both of us—we made that!" (Sarah)

"Knowing that you are working together as a team to shape and mold a human being in the best way you know how can be a real bonding experience." (Wendy)

When you realize you are on the same team, it can be a bonding experience. But for most couples it's a process to *grow through* to become a team. We are on a team together, but sometimes we look more like arch rivals as we battle over "my" way or "his" way.

making the percentages work

After we (Sharon and Pat) had our first child, we found ourselves on opposing teams, like a pair of elementary kids playing tug-of-war. He would give 50 percent of "umph" to our marriage, and I mirrored his efforts. As long as I was only offering 50 percent to our marriage, I had half of my time to look and see what he *wasn't doing* for *me*. His 50 percent was not the 50 percent I would have chosen for him to be doing, and what I was giving wasn't the 50 percent he would have chosen for me to contribute either. But 50 plus 50 equals 100, right? Not in marriage.

My husband's effort included bringing home a paycheck (which was plenty in his eyes, and honestly, I took his efforts for granted), while I saw all the laundry and housework that had taken second place to the needs of our children. I was thinking, *I need your help, and you're not helping enough.* He told me over and over that no matter how much he helped, he thought it would never be enough to please me.

My 50 percent included taking care of children, some housework, preparing meals, but as you know, in those early years it's hard to get much done other than taking care of the baby. Because of all my hard work I felt I deserved to be taken out to dinner—lots!—but my practical husband saw that the budget couldn't afford meals out on such a frequent basis. In short, our interpretations of the whole situation were as different as oil and water.

We soon realized that to be on the same team it would take *both* of us giving *100* percent to the endeavor. When I'm giving 100 percent I don't really have time to think about what my husband *isn't* doing. Remember the goals and desires from chapter 9? All we as wives can really control is our 100 percent.

Who comes first in your family? In mine, it's often the kid that is screaming the loudest! Early in our marriage I cared about my husband's needs and always wanted to be with him, but I had come to the point where I sometimes forgot to get him something to drink with his dinner.

I was so focused on our kids that he finally told me one night, after the kids were asleep, "I really don't have to be at the top of the totem pole. But can I just be moved up a few notches?"

I felt horrible. I'm not satisfied with my husband moving up a few notches on the totem pole. He needs and deserves to be at the *top* of my list. And our children need to see that he is my top priority. As we have added more children, I find that it's a constant battle for me to keep my husband at the top.

What about you? Where is your husband on the totem pole? Is he at the top, with you talking to your kids about how much you appreciate what he does? Or is your husband hanging around at the bottom of the pole, seen as the guy who can never do enough?

When we treat them like that, they tend to find ways to stay away from us—working long hours all the time, hanging out with the guys, spending their time on the computer, going to sporting events, or burying their heads in the newspaper. If we don't appreciate our husbands, we are robbing ourselves as well as the rest of our family of something vital. Staying on the same team involves making him a top priority, even when you don't think he deserves it. It's a choice we make.

team strategies

If I choose not to talk to my husband (the silent treatment) or he just lets things burn inside of him, we become enemies, not teammates. What a miserable place to be! But most likely we've all been there. God's plan is for us to be on a unified team. The Bible says, "Two are better than one, because they have a good return for their work: If one falls down, his friend can help him up. . . . Though one may be overpowered, two can defend themselves" (Ecclesiastes 4:9–10, 12).

Just as being on any team takes practice, marriage is no different. It's easy for us as moms to become so wrapped up in the kids that we don't make our marriage a priority. Making your husband a top priority lets him know that you *want* to be on his team. Every team has strategies and plays that help them work together. Here are some marriage "plays" that you can implement to help create a team atmosphere in your home.

what can you do to make his day a little better?

If I am focused on what my husband isn't doing for me, it will be hard for me to do anything nice for him. Sometimes when I'm disgruntled with my husband I make myself do something kind for him. I ask the question, "What can I do to *make* his day a little better?" Immediately I'm focusing on something I can do for him rather than concentrating on what he has neglected to do for me.

Often a simple thing like putting his shoes away or picking up his underwear from the middle of the floor (without my mentioning it to him) can change my perspective of him. Do you think that could work for you? Try it! But don't expect him to notice what you did. The point isn't that he recognize your good deed but that you change your attitude of resentment to one of love for him. (There are practical ways to do this in "Making the Most of the Moments" at the end of this chapter.)

ask for help *before* you are angry

The scene: It's Sunday afternoon and we've just eaten a home-cooked meal (made by me). We're looking forward to a quiet afternoon, and yet before the quiet afternoon can begin, there are dishes to be done. My husband eats, might even say "thank you" for the meal, and then makes his way to his chair and his Sunday newspaper. I sit at the table stunned, thinking, *Surely he is going to help me with the dishes. After all, I prepared the meal. It's obvious (to me) that he should help with the dishes, right?* I begin clearing the table; then as I begin loading the dishwasher, my actions become noticeably exaggerated (at least to me). *If I bang these pots and pans loud enough, he will hear and come and help me.*

When he doesn't come to my aid, I stomp my way to his side, glare at him, and blurt, "I slaved in the kitchen to make this lunch for YOU (never mind the rest of the people in our family that ate the meal). The least you could do is help me with the dishes (or play with the kids while I clean the kitchen so I'm not stepping over, around, or on them)!" This is so motivating to my husband that he stands to his feet and apologizes profusely for his obvious neglect. Ha—you know that's not true! All my fussing just makes him angry. Imagine that!

This scenario played over and over in our home in a variety of settings, always ending with my feeling like the victim, becoming angry, and griping at him, followed by his becoming angry at me. Thus the silent treatment would begin and we would both suffer through the effects of it the rest of the day. Sounds like a winning team, huh?

Many would-be pleasant Sunday afternoons came and went before I finally realized that he wasn't doing this on purpose. My husband is the smartest man I know, but he was *oblivious* to what seemed *obvious* to me. We are just made to think differently. He didn't set out to neglect me every weekend. That is totally against his nature. He would never intentionally hurt me. Washing the dishes just wasn't the first thing on his mind.

One Sunday as we were eating our lunch, I asked, "Honey, would you mind helping me with the dishes after lunch?" To my absolute shock and amazement, he was very willing to help. I couldn't believe it! He got up from the table and started washing dishes. So many Sunday afternoons had been spoiled simply because I hadn't asked for help before I was angry.

I wondered if asking him for help before I was angry would work in other areas. It did! I found that he doesn't mind helping with most any cleaning that needs to be done or anything the kids need *if I ask him in a respectful way*. If I needed help from a stranger, I'd be thoughtful enough to ask for help without becoming angry. Why should my husband be any different?

I remember a situation with a friend of mine who was married with grown children. She would go to the grocery store and then begin to bring the groceries into the house while her husband and grown sons just sat around, letting her do the work. I was appalled and made a promise to myself that I would never let that happen to me. But it did happen to me, and I realized again that I needed to ask for help before I was angry.

My friend never asked for help. She just did it, and had something else to be upset about. But I've learned how to use this important principle. Before I get home from the grocery store, I call my husband to let him know I'm on the way and ask him if he would please meet me at the door to help unload the groceries. He doesn't mind; in fact, he is thrilled I call ahead to ask for help! He told me, "Just like the kids need a five-minute warning before it's time to leave McDonald's, that five-minute warning when you call ahead lets me finish what I'm doing so I can be ready to help."

The key: Ask him for help *before* you're angry. Then . . . after you have asked him for help, remember to take the next important step for building a strong team.

respect his way of doing things

When your husband helps you with a task, he probably won't do it the same way you would. That doesn't mean his way is *wrong,* just *different.* Respect *his way of doing things.*

When he does clean the kitchen, know ahead of time that the kitchen counters probably won't be wiped off and the leftover food might still be left out. If he does put it in the fridge, more than likely he won't cover it up. If pots and pans were used to prepare the meal, just smile when you see them still on the stove waiting for you. (Pots and pans aren't real dishes, you know!)

After speaking to thousands of women across the country, we've learned that it's not just *your* husband who cleans this way. For the most part, all guys will make sure there are plates and forks to eat with next time, but they may not do more than that. Knowing this new tidbit of information (that guys everywhere don't wipe down the counters, don't wash pots and pans, and don't refrigerate the leftovers) can help you. Instead of fussing at him, you can laugh and think, *Isn't that "cute"? He's like most other guys across America!*

Otherwise, you'll get mad at him and forget to thank him for his effort. One of the sound men who heard us speaking on this topic came up to us afterwards and said, "I'll try to help my wife, and think I've done a good job, but she has a radar, only seeing what I didn't do!" When we fuss about *how* they do a job when they were trying to be helpful, it encourages them to go back and watch TV or read the newspaper rather than help. Tell him "thank you" for what he did, even if you have to bite your tongue because you want to tell him how he could have done it better.

Cleaning the kitchen isn't the only time it's important to respect his way of doing things. If you have children who still need help with their bath, know that your husband isn't going to bathe them like you do. He might even get water in their eyes. You may want to intervene, but remember: He *is* helping, and your children *will* survive! He won't feed them what you would, or even burp a baby the way you would. One day as I listened through the baby monitor, I heard Pat rhythmically tapping our baby on the back, trying to get him to burp to the theme song from *I Dream of Jeannie.* I would never have thought to do that, but it worked!

Be especially respectful when he disciplines the kids differently than you would. I sometimes forget that God gave our children *both of us* as parents. This must mean that we bring different things to the role. Unless your husband is abusing your children, remind yourself that they need to learn from him just as they need to learn from you. If we are constantly disagreeing with him in front of the children, the kids are smart enough to figure out how they can play us against each other. That makes it doubly hard to stay on the same team.

It took me a long time to figure this out, but now I can look back and see that my husband has brought balance to our home. If I had continued to show disrespect toward his way of raising our children I would have missed the opportunity to learn from him, and my kids would have missed out on a more structured and balanced home. Sometimes it helps to just . . .

zip my lips

My daughter tells me, "Mommy, when I wanna say something mean, I'm just gonna zip my lips." As wives, there are plenty of times we can do the same. "Set a guard over my mouth, O Lord; keep watch over the door of my lips" (Psalm 141:3). How many disagreements would never turn into fights if we would just keep our mouths shut?

This doesn't mean using "the silent treatment" on our husbands. Refusing to speak is usually driven by pride or repressed anger. We may think our anger is hidden, but it's there, simmering just below the surface. Or we may choose to "stuff" legitimate feelings that need to be aired, and that's not healthy either. There are times that we need to respectfully discuss what's bothering us. But let's be choosy about what issues are important enough to complain about.

The time to zip our lips is when we are tempted to fuss about something that we know doesn't amount to a hill of beans (like what shoes he wears or which route he takes to get to a restaurant). Why create conflict over something as trivial as that? The zip-lip play is one strategy that works great in keeping the team together!

go on dates and getaways

"Take a weekend break! Swap kids with a friend [take turns sitting each other's kids], enlist grandparents, whatever it takes! Nothing sparks the romance like twenty-four hours away from having children climbing all over you!" (Kathy)

At a recent "Mom ... and Loving It" conference, the emcee was giving out door prizes. This particular door prize (a free night at a nice hotel) was going to the mom who had gone the longest without going away overnight with her husband. She started with one year, then as she jumped to five years almost the whole audience was seated. With only a few ladies standing, she kept going. Finally one lone mom was still standing. When asked how long it had been, the sweet woman shared that she had not been anywhere with her husband overnight for eleven years!

Maybe that's you. Maybe it's been longer. There are lots of moms who feel that it would be wrong to leave their children overnight with someone else. What they don't realize is that husbands and wives *need* uninterrupted time together; not only do they need a break from the kids on occasion, but kids also need a break from them!

"The main (only) way Greg and I get to keep the romance in our marriage is by getting out on an occasional date, and by getting away on trips (usually every winter for a week), but also for a weekend. We REALLY appreciate the grandparents who fill in!" (Diane)

Times away are a regular part of our lives as busy moms. If possible, we go on a date with our husbands once a week, and we try to go on an overnight trip together twice a year. We have found that one night is too short, so we take two nights together if we can. After two nights, we often end up really connecting on the way home.

Don't expect your husband to always plan the date. It's fine if you have to call the baby-sitter, reserve a hotel, or schedule dinner with friends. If we expect our husbands to plan everything, we might be setting ourselves up for disappointment.

My daughter once asked me why I (Sharon) go on dates with Daddy. I told her, "Daddy is for keeps. You'll grow up and go away, but Daddy stays!" We're a team, and teams need time to plan and get to know each other better. Almost every mom we talked to, when asked about her marriage and how to keep the romance alive after kids, said: "Go on dates." We all need "connect" time, when we're not just dispatching information about the latest report card, what's for dinner, or what time the game starts. Dates and overnight getaways give you that time to refocus on each other—the original founders of your family. (You'll find creative getaway and date ideas at the end of this chapter.)

the seventy-times-seven principle

We started this chapter with numbers—how fifty plus fifty doesn't cut it in a marriage commitment. Well, Jesus also used math when He was talking to His disciples about forgiveness. "At that point Peter got up the nerve to ask, 'Master, how many times do I forgive a brother or sister who hurts me? Seven?'" (Matthew 18:21–22 THE MESSAGE). I wonder if Peter was expecting Jesus to say, "Oh no, seven is too many. Five times is plenty. Wow, Peter! If you can forgive seven times, that's amazing—way to go!" Peter had to be thinking, *Who would really deserve to be forgiven seven times over? I mean, surely they would get a clue after a couple of times.* But Jesus startled him with His response: "Seven? Hardly! Try seventy times seven."

Peter isn't the only one who was floored by that response. Sometimes I am overwhelmed by the graciousness of such a statement. The thought that Jesus will forgive not just 490 times but will continue to forgive my sin *infinitely* is astounding. I am amazed and grateful for His unconditional, forgiving love.

But the next thought is, "Am I supposed to forgive someone over and over—as many times as they offend me?" That's a tough one! I've read that verse hundreds of times, heard sermons on it, and pondered it in my mind, but I was at a loss to determine who could possibly offend me 490 times, or seventy times, or even seven times. I always thought of a neighbor down the street, a friend at church, the sour-faced server at a restaurant, or the telemarketer who calls in the middle of dinner over and over. In my mind the possibility was always someone "out there." But none of those people, I decided, could ever hurt my feelings, make me mad, insult me, or upset me *that* many times. I was about to decide that the principle didn't apply to me.

But one night a few months ago I read that verse again, and suddenly I knew the answer! I had discovered the relationship that *could* require my forgiveness so many times I would lose count. Think of all the dirty underwear you've picked up. What about almost falling into the commode in the middle of the night because the lid was left up? The piles of stuff that he leaves behind that can send you into orbit? And think about the words that can cut so deeply. Or maybe it's the lack of words. You long for him to talk to you, to share his life with you, but he seems more interested in his computer or the next game, and your heart breaks—again, and again, and again. Seventy times seven.

Am I really supposed to forgive my husband for those things, Lord? His answer is yes. The Bible says, "Bear with each other and forgive whatever grievances you may have against one another. Forgive as the Lord forgave you. Let the peace of Christ rule in your hearts . . . and be thankful" (Colossians 3:13, 15). Our husbands (and our children as well) are capable of needing our forgiveness infinitely, just as we need that kind of forgiveness from God. And why wouldn't we give it? Do you know what happens when we choose to fuss about every little thing that bothers us? First, our husbands usually don't change (and if they do, it's with some measure of resentment toward us). And second, if we choose not to forgive, we become bitter and hateful toward our husbands.

Many of you have suffered from hurts far deeper than the potty lid being left up. You may have been through divorce, unfaithfulness, abuse, or any number of hurtful scenarios. Though forgiveness is hard in those situations, it can come, but it takes time to rebuild trust again.

For some of us, it's the petty stuff that we have a hard time forgiving. We find ourselves chronically irritated with our husbands for little things like driving the car on empty, forgetting the date of our anniversary, or keeping an immaculate yard while his car looks like a pigsty! When you and I choose to forgive, we can enjoy life with our husbands instead of always griping at them.

I wrote in my Bible beside Matthew 18, "God has forgiven me for so much, yet I'm sometimes slow to forgive pettiness." You can't control what your husband chooses to do, but by forgiving him you release yourself from those emotions that can bind you. When someone needs your forgiveness, it automatically means they don't *deserve* it. They might not have asked you to forgive them, but if you were hurt, offended, embarrassed, or insulted, it's your choice to forgive them. Your decision to forgive frees you to love them even when they don't deserve it. In this way we identify with Jesus, who freely forgave us when we did not deserve it either.

Staying on the same team is crucial to successful marriages. We can make our team stronger by keeping our husbands at the top of the totem pole, finding things that will make his day better, asking him for help before we're angry, respecting his way of doing things, zipping our lips, making time to connect, and forgiving him again and again. Go team!

First Corinthians 13:4–8 (THE MESSAGE)

Love never gives up.
Love cares more for others than for self.
Love doesn't want what it doesn't have.
Love doesn't strut,
Doesn't have a swelled head,
Doesn't force itself on others,
Isn't always "me first,"
Doesn't fly off the handle,
Doesn't keep score of the sins of others,
Doesn't revel when others grovel,
Takes pleasure in the flowering of truth,
Puts up with anything,
Trusts God always,
Always looks for the best,
Never looks back,
But keeps going to the end.
Love never dies.

stop, drop, and restore your soul

When you got married, you were probably silly in love, anxious to begin your life with "the one." You had finally found him!

1. How has your relationship changed since children entered the picture?
2. How do you keep the romance alive? Or are you like the woman who said, "Romance, what's that?"
3. Do you feel like you are on the same team, or do you feel more like arch rivals?
4. What "marriage plays" do you need to work on to build your team?

Father,

I know You've seen us play tug-of-war. You've seen me skimp and only give fifty percent because I thought my husband's efforts were feeble and halfhearted. Help me to notice when he does help and remind me to thank him for it. Show me when I need to ask for his help, and help me to be respectful when I ask. When I need to zip my lip, set a guard over my mouth, Lord. Help me not to argue over silly things that don't really matter. Instead, fill me with love for my husband, love that is unconditional and forever. Help me to find creative ways to love and romance him. And help me to forgive him when he doesn't deserve it. I want Your best, Lord, for our team, the team that You have put together. I pray in the mighty name of Jesus. Amen.

making the most of the moments

1. **what can i do for you?** Here are some ideas to change your focus from what your husband is not doing to what you can do for him to make his day better. He might not notice, but that's okay. You do it in love for the purpose of changing *your* thoughts about him:

   Call his parents, just because.
   Make up the bed.
   Put a glass in the freezer for him so he can have an ice-cold drink.
   Call a baby-sitter so you can have a surprise night out together.
   Use dry-erase markers to write a note to him on the bathroom mirror.
   Leave a note taped to his cell phone or the steering wheel.
   Put a Hershey's kiss in his pants pocket, and make sure he finds it before it melts!

2. **creative getaways and dates**

   House Swap Switch houses with a friend overnight. The reason is that if you send your kids to their house, and the two of you stay home, you'll want to clean. So let the friends stay with your kids at your house and you two go to their house.

   Cousin Swap Our brother has kids the same ages as our kids, so we combine the three families of kids, and during the summer each couple takes all the kids overnight to give the other couples a getaway time. Work one cousin swap, get two free—quite the deal!

Surprise! Tell him not to plan anything for the evening, then pack his bag, get a sitter, and go to a hotel. Check out *hotwire.com* or *priceline.com* for a reasonable getaway package.

Let's Go Parkin'! Go to a restaurant and take the back way home ... remember parking?

The Ball Is in Your Court Play tennis or some other recreational sport you enjoyed before your kids came along.

Wanna Play? Play a board game or work a puzzle together.

House Arrest Our friends Michael and Amy reserve a night to sit on the couch and watch their favorite TV show. No computers or phones are allowed—just being there together on the "love seat." Another friend (Tammy) shared about their "at-home" date night: "We put the kids to bed, order one meal, with an extra salad or order of bread, from a nice restaurant. When you share one meal and have your drinks at home, and don't have to pay a baby-sitter, it really saves a lot of money! We rent a movie or two and just camp out in the living room for the evening."

Keep Walking Go for a walk. If your kids are small, get a trusted neighbor to watch them or take them in a stroller with you. Great dates don't have to cost money.

3. **zip it!** "Set a guard over my mouth, O Lord; keep watch over the door of my lips" (Psalm 141:3). I wrote this verse down and put it everywhere because this is a particular struggle of mine. My kids struggle with their words too, so I let them draw pictures of the verse. Guards posted beside lip doors can make quite a funny picture, but it sure helps illustrate the point!

4. **pray without ceasing** Pray for your husband—your teammate—throughout the day. Ask God to help you pray effectively for him. This means you will need to know what special challenges he is facing at the moment. It's hard to be mad at someone you're praying for. In fact, it might be just the thing to make you fall in love with him all over again.

chapter eleven

being content with your kids
Just the Way They Are!

---

*My first child was like an angel straight from heaven. He
was so easy in every way that my husband and I were
convinced we must be the best authorities on child rearing. I
wanted to write a book on raising the perfect child. Then
God sent us our second son, and I bought every book
on child rearing I could find!*

Janet

**O Lord, you have searched my children and you know them.... For
you created their inmost being; you knit them together in the womb.**

(PSALM 139:1, 13 [LAURIE'S PARAPHRASE])

Why can't you just be still?" you plead with your son, who has more
energy than the Energizer bunny. He keeps on going and going!
"Look at Sam," you say, "he sits quietly at the table while he colors, and
you can't be still for two minutes." Or maybe you have a very shy child,
one who clings to your leg, causing you to walk as if you were dragging
a ball and chain. You long for your child to be more outgoing. You wish
he would *speak up* when spoken to, but all he can do is bury his head
somewhere further behind you. "Why can't you be more outgoing and
speak up like Susie?" you ask. "She talks to everyone. She is so friendly."
But if you happen to be the mother of Susie, you wish she would just
shut up, because she talks nonstop! Isn't it true that we can easily become
discontented with who our children are, longing for them to be different
in some way?

The struggle goes even deeper for those moms with special-needs
kids (SNK). The hopes and desires they have for their children are many

times shattered soon after the birth of their child. Their children really are "different," and it seems *everyone* notices. Nan, a mom of a twenty-one-year-old son with Down's syndrome, says, "The dream of a perfect, normal child has to die. You're not going to get that, so now you have to realize the dream for *this* child."

Joy, the mother of four-year-old twins disabled from premature birth, told us:

> I remember very clearly the circumstances that brought me to accept the fact that our family would never be "normal." While my husband and I were dining out at a restaurant one night, I observed a family sitting at an adjacent table. Two preschool-age children were talking with their parents and having a great time. I began to feel anxious as a myriad of questions were passing through my mind, *Will our daughter learn to talk? Will our son gain enough coordination so that he could eat in public without a mess? Will they ever be potty-trained, so we don't have to worry about dirty diapers when we go out?* Even though I was aware of the special needs we were currently facing with our twins, I guess in the back of my mind I held out hope that someday it would all go away and our family could be what everyone calls "normal."

Several years ago I (Laurie) was struggling with one of my kids in particular. For some reason everything this child did grated on my nerves like fingernails on a chalkboard. I had just assumed that I would do the same things with her that I had done with my son and get the same results. The only problem was, she was *different*. I tried and tried to press her into *his* mold and she wasn't fitting very well. Imagine that! It seemed the harder I tried to make her conform the more she resisted, and conflict would follow.

As my daughter became more independent and her personality began to blossom, the war was on between us. No matter what I laid out for her to wear, she wanted to wear something else. After asking me to help her with her hair, she'd decide she didn't like it, which meant doing it again. She was never still, always doing little things that drove me crazy. Because I couldn't figure out the make of her mold, I struggled in our relationship. I considered her to be a difficult, challenging child, and many times I prayed that God would change her.

I was constantly on her case, griping at her about insignificant things, becoming annoyed by her mannerisms, and relentlessly picking apart everything she did. Little by little I was chipping away at her sensitive spirit. I remember feeling justified in what I would critically spew all over her, until I would hear the tone of my voice and see the look on her face.

The guilt I was experiencing weighed heavier day by day. I knew I was breaking her spirit, but couldn't seem to stop the negative merry-go-round I was on. Over and over I would tell myself, "Laurie, you've got to stop being so hard on her. She is going to hate you if you keep this up." I would try my best to be encouraging. "I'm only going to use positive words with her," I would tell myself, and for a while that would work. But temporary success provided little hope when it was so quickly followed by the same failures.

As I went to ask my daughter for forgiveness (again), I knew she had forgiven me, but I desired to be free from the bondage of the negative cycle I was in. I had tried everything but still felt hopeless and helpless to make long-term changes in my words and actions.

I keenly remember the day it happened. She came bouncing into my room and had something really exciting to tell me. I was busy making my bed and instead of looking into her eyes and *really* listening to her exciting story, I glanced up and noticed that she had her dirty feet on the wall. All the self-control I had that day flew out the window.

I interrupted her story and flew into her with my usual criticism, "Get your feet off my wall! How many times have I told you not to put your feet on the wall? The floor is for feet, not the wall! Why can't you remember that?" She stood there for a minute, forgetting the rest of her story. She looked at me with a face that said, "I can't do anything right; I've disappointed you again, Mommy." She turned and walked away with her head hanging low, her step slowed, and her spirit broken.

The guilt I felt that day was unbearable. I literally fell to the floor sobbing as I cried out to God, "Why did you make me a mom? I can't do this. It's too hard. I'm a complete failure, Lord. Why did you choose me to be her mom?" At that moment I felt that anyone else in the whole world could do a better job at mothering than me. "I don't deserve her," I cried out.

My heart was broken. I had tried everything I knew to do. I felt completely hopeless. But it was in that moment of desperation that God's

Spirit gently spoke to me, saying, "Laurie, I created her inside and out, and I created you; and I know you both better than you know your-selves. I *chose* you to be her mom, and her to be your child. I have a plan and purpose for your lives, and I didn't make a mistake."

I responded, "But Lord, surely it is not your plan for me to crush her spirit with my critical, negative attitude. I've tried to stop, and I can't. I just can't do it! What is wrong with me?" He patiently spoke again, "Laurie, I created her just like I want her to be. I know her far better than you do." Suddenly I had a glimmer of hope as I thought, *God, since You made her inside and out, You can give me insight into who she is and what makes her tick, can't You?* With a renewed hope I prayed, *"Lord, give me Your eyes to see her the way You do."*

seeing my child through God's perspective

Though nothing had changed in my circumstances, God had changed my perspective *about* my circumstances. He had restored my hope for an encouraging future. Jeremiah 29:11–13 says, "'For I know the plans I have for you,' declares the Lord, 'plans to prosper you and not to harm you, plans to give you *hope* and a *future*. Then you will call upon me and come and pray to me, and I *will* listen to you. You will seek me and *find* me when you seek me with all your heart'" (emphasis added). It wasn't all up to me. I had God's Spirit living in me, who could super-naturally give me insight into the life of my child.

I began to pray, "Lord, give me Your eyes to see her the way You do" on a daily basis. And slowly I began to see changes. One day, about two weeks later I remember playing a game with my daughter. The thought flitted through my mind, *I'm having so much fun with her . . . and there is no conflict. Wow, she is so much fun! Thank you, God, for changing her.* God quickly reminded me that it wasn't my daughter He was chang-ing, it was *me!* I swiftly changed my prayer of thanks to "Thank You, Father, for changing me."

Have you been there? It seems that there is usually one child who becomes the family scapegoat. Maybe you know what it is like because you were one in your family. It is a common struggle for parents to have a hard time with one child in particular, but with God's insight there is hope for change.

God was *really* helping me to see my daughter differently. I began to focus not so much on the outward things that didn't really matter but instead looked deeper—to her heart. God was so gracious to show me times when I just needed to keep my mouth shut, not saying anything, when before I would have been all over her. I began to accept her for *who she was* and not so much *who I wanted her to be*. God opened my eyes to see what a wonderful person He had created, just the way she was!

Sometimes it can seem that those challenging kids do things just to drive us nuts! One mom described her hard-to-deal-with child:

> I have been blessed with a sweet little girl. However, I sometimes wonder what goes through her mind. From her actions, I think it might be the following:
>
> • Let's see what the new baby does when I jab my finger in her eye.
>
> • How would this chicken nugget taste if I completely cover it in salt?
>
> • I wonder how long it takes to let the water out of the five-gallon cooler?
>
> • These postage stamps make really neat stickers.
>
> • I think the baby is hungry. Maybe she'd like a piece of celery.
>
> • I bet chocolate handprints would improve the look of this couch.
>
> • It is impossible for me to keep my shoes on if I am in my car seat.
>
> • I need to be on top of the highest appliance in the house.
>
> • Every object in this house needs my signature on it in permanent marker.
>
> • Diaper wipes look so lonely in that box. I should take them all out so they can play.
>
> • I wonder if this green marker is as healthy as green vegetables.
>
> • Mom's hair stuff smells good. I should rub it all over my body.
>
> • Jumping from the couch to the coffee table needs to be an Olympic event.
>
> • Sleep is for sissies!
>
> • My goal in life is to take everything within my reach and put it where it doesn't belong.

• I wonder what the word *no* means? My mommy sure says it a lot!

Mothering this child is challenging for me. It seems I am constantly picking up after her, cleaning her messes, or rescuing her from
her latest mishap. It's exhausting! I feel like I am forever telling her
"stop," "quit," or "don't." I get angry with her sometimes. "Why
does she do these things?" I ask myself. "Will she ever stop?" In the
end I may never know why and can only hope she'll stop. I have
searched for answers in how to parent her and have come up with
only one solution. Follow God's example and just love her as He
loves me when I make mistakes and messes. (Ann)

If you are struggling with one of your children, start praying that
God would give you His eyes to see that child the way He does. God
sees straight into our children's hearts when we, with our human eyes,
tend to see those outer things that can sometimes drive us crazy. I love 1
Samuel 16:7. It says, " 'The Lord does not look at the things man looks
at. Man looks at the outward appearance, but the Lord looks at the
heart.' " I need God's balance. I need *His* perspective on my children,
because, on my own, I tend to focus on the negative.

precious in His sight

All children may be precious in *His* sight but not always in *ours!* And
all children are different. One mom describes,

My firstborn was such an easy baby. He relished a schedule.
When he went on solid food, he even pooped at the same time every
day! He was orderly with his toys as a preschooler. I just thought I
was the best, most organized mom. Then came baby number two!
There was no schedule. She hated order. Her toys were constantly
mixed up and everywhere. But she is a natural born leader and very
bright. I am praying, however, that she will always be able to afford
a maid! (Brandye)

Remember the mom of twins with special needs? God also changed
her perspective of her children. She shared the conclusion of her story
and how God helped her accept her children for who He made them to
be:

As I discussed it with my husband later that night, my panic at the restaurant about wanting to be a "normal" family, I realized that I had to forget about the word *normal*. I had been using the world's terminology to decide what was acceptable and what was not. After all, our family is not "abnormal" in God's sight! It is perfectly normal in God's eyes, because this is exactly how He planned it. We can be content as long as we are in the center of God's will for *us*. If we set expectations of our family based on someone else's standards, we are bound to be disappointed and unhappy. For the parent of a special-needs child, finding contentment can be a daily challenge. However, it is possible when we keep our eyes focused *above* and not on others around us. There we will find peace and contentment as we trust and rest in His plans for our lives.

insight into their world

As God began to open my eyes to see as He does, He gave me insight into my daughter's world. He helped me to understand what made her tick, what she needed from me. When we seek God's insight, He is faithful to answer. Jan, a stepmom, shared about her challenging step-daughter:

> God showed me how much He loves us in all our uniqueness. The funny thing is, I sometimes see glimpses of myself in this child, and I very much remember what it was like *not* to have an understanding, patient adult in my life, that someone who would encourage me in my gifts. That is probably what drives me to accept, love, and nurture her more than anything.

Gary Chapman and Ross Campbell, in their book *The Five Love Languages of Children,*[1] identify five specific "love languages" or love needs that children have: touch and affection, gifts, words of encouragement, quality time, and acts of service.

As I learned about these, it suddenly hit me—my daughter's love language was touch and affection. One of the things that would drive me crazy about her was the fact that she was like a dryer sheet stuck to my pants. She was constantly longing to be near me, always touching me, rubbing on me, and sitting so close to me that I thought I would suffocate. Sometimes I caught myself gasping for breath as I would move away from her because I felt smothered.

One day I thought, *If her love language is touch and affection, then maybe*

I need to initiate *touch and affection in her life.* So even though it was the last thing I wanted to do, I set out to "beat her to the touch." This proved to be a challenge since she had a little sister who had my lap most of the time.

But I was determined to see if my *initiating* touch and affection in her life would make a difference in how we related to one another. I began instigating loving touch every time I had an opportunity. I would grab her hand (before she grabbed mine), rub her back, stroke her hair when she was standing next to me, paint her fingernails, etc.—whatever I could think of to provide touch and affection in her life.

It was thrilling to see the changes in her behavior. She was no longer adhering to me like Cling Wrap. She seemed more relaxed, more comfortable with who she was, not always questioning her appearance and abilities. Before this she constantly asked, "Mommy, do you think this looks good? Did I do my hair good? I don't think I did very well on my picture." I felt that she was questioning her abilities because she didn't feel that I was pleased with who she was or what she did. Looking back, she reminded me of a small, fragile flower whose tender petals I'd withered by my harsh words. But I now watched her confidence blossom and flourish as I learned to shower her with the nourishment she needed . . . love and acceptance of how God made her!

You might be thinking, *I would love to speak my child's love language, but I have no idea how to figure out what it is.* Here are some thoughts that might help you get started in the right direction and give you insight into your child: Think about what your child enjoys doing the most. Ask yourself, "What do they frequently do for me or say to me?" Notice what you say or do that makes their eyes light up.

If your child constantly makes you things, or brings you "treasures" (things like bugs, bottle tops, rocks, pieces of metal), you may have a child with the love language of *gifts.* How do you speak this child's love language? Love them by giving them gifts. Not expensive ones, just a little something that says, "I was thinking of you and love you." It could be as simple as your finding a pretty rock you know they would appreciate, making or buying them a card, or giving them a flower.

On the other hand, if your child is constantly asking you, "Mom, do you like my picture?" or "Did you see that great play I made in the second quarter?" then you may have a child who is a *words of encourage-*

ment kid. These kids need lots of positive verbal affirmation from you. Try to encourage them before they ask for it!

Quality time kids usually love it when you stop to spend one-on-one time with them. They also get really excited about a family craft or project. My son, Alec, really appreciates it when our whole family can go outside and play tag or some other game together. If your son or daughter is into computer games, Playstation or Xbox, sit down and let them teach you how to play. Sometimes simply sitting by them while they are playing the game fills their emotional tank up enough to save you from the humiliation of complete annihilation if you actually try to play the game.

Maybe your child is always doing things for you. They may sneak into your bedroom and make your bed, only to surprise you later by making you close your eyes as they hold your hand and drag you to see what they've done. Then on their cue (and not a moment before) they yell with excitement, "Open your eyes!" as if it were an episode of *Trading Spaces*. Then they watch your face to see how you will respond to their act of service. You'd best act excited or you'll be in big trouble. If you have had this or a similar "surprise" in your home, you probably have an *acts of service* kind of child. They are the kids who love it when you offer to do a chore for them when they least expect it.

For the *touch and affection* kids, they need lots of hugs. They usually like to snuggle. They can be very curious and love to touch and feel things. For this child it is sometimes a challenge to speak their love language because it is the last thing you want to do. You may already feel smothered by their affection. However, if you can initiate touch and affection in their lives, you may, like me, be surprised to find that they don't demand it of you as much.

putting it into action

Discovering a child's (husband's, mother-in-law's, co-worker's) love language is an incredible tool that can be used to make daily activities and relationships more bearable, maybe even peaceful. Mornings at our home were a struggle. It seemed that my daughter was allergic to them. She broke out in an unbearably negative attitude each day when it was time to get up. She would whine, complain, and argue until I would become frustrated and begin making threats (you know, the ones that really made her want to wake up with a happy heart). I just hated starting our day out in a fuss, but she had to get up, right?

One morning I thought, *You know, Laurie, her love language is touch and affection, so why don't you try using it?* So the next morning I went quietly to her bed, scooped my arm under her sleeping body, and hugged her up close to me. I kissed her on her forehead and then laid my cheek against hers. She rolled over toward me, kissed me on the cheek, and threw her arms around my neck. With a smile on my face I said, "Good morning, sweetie. It's time to get up." I held her for a few seconds longer and then she rolled out of bed without a hint of whining. I was in complete shock—I couldn't believe it really worked. I thought, *Surely this is just a fluke! I'm sure it won't work tomorrow.* But it *did* work the next day, and the next, and the next!

I (Sharon) was having a hard time waking my daughter up too. So I decided to try what Laurie was doing with Abby. Only problem was, Brittlea's love language was *not* touch and affection. But I'm a little slow at times and decided to try it anyway. The first morning I climbed up to the top bunk, scooped my daughter up, and almost got shoved off the bed as she protested, "Stoooop!" If your love language isn't touch and affection, being hugged in the morning is annoying. I decided, *Maybe this isn't going to work.*

I knew I could best love her by giving her *quality time*, but how do you spend quality time with someone who is asleep? Then I had the idea, "Maybe I could read her a book to wake her up." So the next morning I tried it. About halfway through the book Brittlea began to stir. By the end of the book she was sitting up, listening to the story. When I finished the book, Brittlea rolled out of bed without complaining and arguing. And it has worked every time I've done it. I'm still amazed!

Maybe you can determine a particular time of day that is most challenging (morning, mealtime, homework time, bedtime). Try implementing their love language during that time in order to avoid the conflict that usually arises. You might be surprised to see your relationship flourish when you learn to speak their love language.

His grace is sufficient

Being a mom who is content with who her kids are can be a real challenge. Like most moms, I become discontented with my children when I look outside of what I have. It helps me when I remember that God is the Creator. He put us together and has a plan and purpose for our lives. God is waiting to give us insight into the hearts of our children, if we will only seek Him.

As moms we can feel utterly defeated and deem ourselves complete failures at this parenting thing, thinking, *God, surely anyone could do a better job than I'm doing today!* It is in these moments I am reminded that without His strength I can't do this job of mothering.

I love the verse in 2 Corinthians 12:9, which says, "My grace is sufficient for you, for my power is made perfect in weakness." As moms we play the "good mom" game: We try to handle everything all on our own, wanting others to think we have it all together. But if we really want to be the best mom to our kids, we need to quit trying to do it all alone and let God be our strength.

God would like to remind us through these child-rearing years that He is in control. He has a plan for our children, and we, as the mommies, play a vital part in it. He knew about the plan for our lives long before we did. Psalm 139:13–16 says it so well, "For you created my inmost being; you knit me together in my mother's womb. I praise you because I am fearfully and wonderfully made; your works are wonderful, I know that full well. My frame was not hidden from you when I was made in the secret place. When I was woven together in the depths of the earth, your eyes saw my unformed body. *All the days ordained for me were written in your book before one of them came to be*" (emphasis added).

He knew the plan before we were born. He didn't make a mistake when He created you or your child. We can be confident in His call on our lives to be mothers, because it isn't our plan we are fulfilling—it is His. So even on those "bad mommy" days you can be confident in God's plan that you are the one. You can do it!

stop, drop, and restore your soul

Because kids can be so different, we need God's vision to see them the way He does. As moms we tend to focus on all the things about our children that annoy us, but God looks past all that and sees straight to their heart! He can open our eyes to see as He does and enable us to love them in their uniqueness.

1. Do you struggle with a challenging child? What are some things that your child does that can sometimes push you "over the edge"?

2. What is your child's love language? How do the things you listed in answer to question 1 relate to their unique personality or love language?

3. How can you change your response to those annoying actions of your child?

4. What is your most challenging time of day? How can you implement your child's love language during that time?

5. How can you see evidence of God giving you *His* eyes to see your child the way He does?

Oh, Father,

I need Your strength and insight so desperately. You know I want the best for my children, but many times my patience is completely spent. Lord, I need Your eyes to see them the way You do. I know You see straight into their hearts, and I am so guilty of getting stuck on the things that don't really matter. Open my eyes to see what really matters to You. Help me to learn to love them the way they need to be loved. You promise that "when I'm weak, You will be strong" ... and I am weak! Thank You, Father, for loving me enough to convict me of my sins, and yet loving me enough to restore me. Teach me Your ways, so that I will be able to teach them to my children. Amen.

making the **most** of the moments

1. **write** Write 1 Samuel 16:7 on index cards and put them up around your house to remind you of what's most important!

2. **drop** When your child is telling you a story, stop what you are doing (if possible), bend down on your knee (unless your child is as tall or taller than you), and look into his/her eyes, not being distracted by where their arms and legs are. Let them know that you care more about what they have to say than what their feet are touching.

3. **be real** If you have older children, talk to them individually about

the struggles you had at their age. Let them know you can relate.

4. **mark** Mark the positive milestones with your child on the calendar or in a journal. You will be able to look back on the challenging days and remember why you are a mom ... and loving it.

5. **read** Take time in the next week to read through Psalm 139, maybe more than once. You might even try memorizing parts of it that particularly speak to you. Let it remind you that you and your children are "fearfully and wonderfully made"!

chapter **twelve**

the power of words
How They Affect Our Kids

Words, words, words—that's all I ever hear.
Brittlea, to her mom (at age three)

Encourage one another and build each other up.
(1 THESSALONIANS 5:11A)

Be gracious in your speech. The goal is to bring out the best in others in a conversation, not put them down, not cut them out.
(COLOSSIANS 4:6 THE MESSAGE)

After a conference a young mom shared something with us. While she was tucking her young son into bed one night she tenderly looked into his eyes and said, "Do you know that we are *so* proud of you?" To her surprise he abruptly responded, "No, you're not!" In shock, she asked, "Why would you say that?" He responded, "Because I don't chew with my mouth closed, I interrupt you when I'm not supposed to, and I can't throw the ball the way Daddy wants me to." He went on to repeat all the ways in which he felt inadequate, how he didn't measure up to their expectations.

Her story really hit home with me. I (Laurie) could easily add a few that my children might use, like "I'm too loud, I can't clean up good enough, I forget to use my manners, I'm too wiggly," etc. Would our kids (yours and mine) believe we are really proud of them, or would the negative tape player of their mind replay all the ways in which they feel inadequate? Do our words "encourage and build up" as the Scripture above says, or do they dishearten and tear down our children's spirits?

James 3:3–7 talks about how powerful the tongue is. "A word out of your mouth may seem of no account, but it can accomplish nearly anything—or destroy it!" (James 3:5 THE MESSAGE). This is not only true in the lives of our children but also with us moms. Sometimes I've found myself feeling much like the little boy, playing the negative tape over and over in my mind. Isn't it true that we hang on to the negative far longer than the positive?

Sharon and I spoke at a large conference for moms a few years ago, and after the conference was over they provided each speaker with evaluation cards filled out by the ladies who attended each workshop. There were probably 150 comments in total, and 98 percent of them were very encouraging and uplifting. Some even spoke of the workshop as something that changed their lives, but what do you think I focused on? Yes, the 2 percent of the comments that weren't glowing. They weren't really critical or negative; mostly they simply offered suggestions for improvement. But I still brooded about them.

I've heard it said that it takes twenty positive comments to every one negative comment to balance the scales of our mind. Words are powerful. If you've worked in the business world, you have probably been trained on how to provide constructive criticism to an employee. They *train* you in the "right way" to tell someone they are messing up. I remember hearing that you should sandwich criticism in between positive comments so that the person will not feel that you are only focusing on the negative. When people believe they are doing something right, instead of everything wrong, they will more readily hear and learn from constructive criticism.

Somehow when we have children, we don't feel the need to follow the same suggestions. We can find ourselves constantly saying, "Don't do that; stop doing that; why aren't you. . . ?" Or, "Why are you. . . ?" forgetting to praise them for who they are and what they are doing right. I have to ask myself, "Is my conversation with my children primarily characterized by criticism and correction?" "Or do the positive comments far outweigh the negative ones?" For me, the answer varies according to the day. With a toddler who is constantly testing the boundaries, praising more than correcting can be a challenge!

Am I saying that we should never correct our children? Absolutely not! When our children are young, it seems that our days are filled with a string of "do not's." That's our job—to correct and direct, particularly in those vulnerable years. But how do we do that without producing in them a negative self-concept? I think the key is knowing the difference between *correcting a behavior* and *attacking a person*. And many times the way we say something makes all the difference in the mind of our children. It's not so much *what we say* but *how we say it*. Maybe these suggestions will help.

become a "yes" mom

If your child frequently says, "Mom, I know you're probably going to say no, but can we . . ." you may be a "no" mom, more negative than positive. It is easy to be one, because our children are tugging for our time all day long. Often I find myself saying no to my child's requests simply because I don't want to stop what I'm doing, I don't feel like it, it isn't a good time, or I'm too tired. Sometimes their request may truly be a bad choice; however, that is usually not the initial reason I say no.

Even in situations that require our saying no to their request, we can usually give our kids a couple of related acceptable options we can live with; letting them choose one of them can help soften the effect of our "no." Your denial can then be used as a teaching opportunity in making good choices. For example, if your child asks to have a cookie before lunch, rather than just saying no, you might say, "You may have a banana now or wait to have your cookie after lunch." For an older child who asks to play on the computer, again, you might suggest they go play outside, read a book, or play a board game. Sometimes all they need is some direction.

How can you be a "yes" mom? One way is to *think* before you automatically say no or yes. Sometimes I tell my kids, "I'm thinking about your question, and I'll give you an answer later." That gives me time to consider, "Is their request something I *can* or *cannot* do, or is it just that I cannot do it *right now*? Could I possibly do it later and give a specific time when I will?" Of course, if I opt for this last possibility, I have to be sure that I follow through with my promise!

One day Abby asked me (Laurie) if we could paint. My first thought was *Ugh, why do they always pick that project?* But instead of mindlessly saying "no" to her request, I said, "I'd love to paint with you, but I need to finish unloading the dishwasher first. Can you help me put the silverware away? Then I'll paint with you for thirty minutes!" She hopped right up to help with the silverware, and then we painted for thirty minutes. She was happy, and so was I.

Sometimes you have to give an absolute no, but usually there is another way to respond. You might be able to say something like, "Sweetie, Mommy can't paint with you right now, but you could sit right here beside me and color." It softens our words to our children and lets them know we love being with them. And at the same time it lets them know the reality of our lives.

When you must say no, try saying it with a *smile*. Remember our story from chapter 5? Sharon was amazed at how much better Brittlea responded to her no when it was accompanied with a smile and kind words.

hush-up and pray

So many times my mouth goes into action before my brain kicks in, and I say things I later regret. If I could only stop, take a deep breath, and think for half a second before drenching my children with my negative thoughts and feelings, I'd do much less damage in my home. The problem is that it probably doesn't come naturally for any of us to think before we speak; it is something we have to have supernatural help with. And with God's help we *can* train our mouths not to say everything we think and feel.

Many times I become angry with my child for things that simply bother me. There may not be anything really *wrong* with what they are doing . . . it just bugs the life out of me! So when I slow down enough to think, I must ask myself, "Is my child's action morally wrong or disrespectful? Are they hurting themselves, other people, or someone else's property?" If not, then do I really need to say something? Could I simply zip my lips and say nothing at all? I love the Scripture in 2 Timothy 2:14 (THE MESSAGE): "Warn them before God against pious nitpicking, which chips away at the faith. It just wears everyone out." Isn't it true that nitpicking wears *everyone* out, even the nitpicker?

One Sunday morning after church I was feeling very powerful in my role as MOTHER. My son had not behaved like I thought he should have in church, and I was determined not to let him get away with his actions. So I let him have it verbally. He was humiliated and angry, and I was irritated.

As I was leaving the auditorium, however, I ran into my friend Mr. Bob. I was still murmuring about my son's misbehavior and how I, in all my authority, was not going to allow my son to behave in such a manner. He looked at me and said, "You know, Laurie, it's not all up to you." A little puzzled, I answered, "Huh?" Unwavering in my stance, I was thinking, *Yes, it is up to me to make him behave. I am the mother!*

But remembering the wisdom of Mr. Bob's advice in the past, I didn't say what I was thinking. I asked, "What do you mean?" He said, "It's not all up to you. You are not the only one responsible for your children's behavior." This time I did ask aloud, "But as the parent isn't it *my* job to train him?"

He replied, "Yes, but not you *alone*. There are three entities that have responsibility. You and Charles, as the parents, Alec, as the child, and since Alec has a relationship with Christ, God holds much power to convict his heart." Stunned, I said, "Oh, I never thought about it that way." Then he said, "Laurie, you don't have to bear the burden alone. There may be times that you don't need to say anything to Alec. Instead, pray that God would convict him of his actions."

I walked away that day with a new awareness of my role as a parent. I felt lighter, knowing it wasn't all up to me. I am not called to be the "Holy Spirit" in my child's life. The Holy Spirit can do that job all by himself. I don't have to nitpick everything my child does. Many times I need to simply zip my lips and pray.

One day, not long after this experience, Alec was acting irresponsibly (like the nine-year-old he was). It was driving me crazy, and I was nagging him. I heard him telling a fib to his cousin, and I started to get on to him before I remembered—*It is not all up to me.* So I turned my back to him and prayed, "Lord, You convict him of this lie. Teach him to take responsibility for his actions and words." When I turned back around, I heard him change his story to the truth. I felt like shouting "Hallelujah!" God convicted him of his sin and I didn't have to. What a great lesson it was for me.

When I realized that it was not all up to me to correct my child's every deviant behavior, a burden was lifted. Now I really felt powerful, knowing that I am on a parenting team far bigger, more influential, and better equipped than the one I'd been on all by myself. God is teaching me to zip my lips, pray, and let Him work in my child's life.

stop the yelling

My husband (Charles) shared with some parents one weekend that he struggled with yelling at the kids when he would see them doing something he didn't approve of. He told them that he was working on calling the kids to come to him, instead of yelling at them from afar. When they would come to him (which would give him a little time to cool off), even though he was angry, he would hold them close, sitting them on his lap. He would then talk to them about their actions. He said, "You just can't yell at a kid who is sitting in your lap." Doesn't that make sense? Neither of us has mastered this model, but we are sure working at it.

There are times when, for a child's safety, you must speak emphatically (yell) to get his or her attention. The problem is that we often use a forceful tone of voice for things that shouldn't require it. If we are constantly yelling at our children, they learn to tune us out. And in a true emergency—when a car is coming or they've wandered too far away—when we need to get their attention, they might not even hear us. As our grandmother says, "Don't be hollerin' all the time . . . save it for when the cows are in the corn" (when there's a true emergency).

introduce your child in a positive manner

Many times we are tempted to introduce our children by mentioning their faults or the things that bug us. For example, you might say something like, "I'd like you to meet my son, Blake. He's our 'wild child'" or "I'd like to introduce you to my daughter; she's a talker (or she's shy, or she's a climber)." Do you see what I mean? It's easy when we are introducing them to use some description that identifies a behavior we've frequently corrected in them. We do it because we want to warn the people we're introducing them to. "BEWARE of this child!"

When Sharon was at a local tire shop she noticed a grandpa who came in with his adorable grandson. The owner of the tire shop said, "Wow, you've got a good-looking young man there with ya!" The grandpa had a wonderful opportunity to encourage that little guy with his kind words, but instead he said, "Oh, he's trouble." If that little boy keeps hearing that, he probably *will* be trouble in a few years. Our words are powerful—to either build up or to tear down. A lady told me one day, "What you say about your children in front of someone else is what they'll *remember*."

As tempting as it may be to introduce your child like the grandpa did, try to think of something encouraging to say. Here are some suggestions: "She has such a sweet spirit; he is very compassionate; she is great with babies; she loves animals; he's a great big brother; she is so flexible." Some of you may have to think about it for a while, but I know God will bring something encouraging to your mind to use when you introduce your child.

Our dad was great at making us feel special. When we were young he would have to make deliveries to Dallas once a week, and when he could he would take one of us kids with him. We loved that "one-on-one" time with our dad. I remember feeling so special riding in that big delivery truck. When we would arrive at the loading docks, Daddy would hold my hand as we entered the building. The guys would always ask, "Hey, Hank, who do you have with you?" He'd reply, "I've got my right-hand man." I didn't care that he was calling me a *man*. All I knew was that my dad was *proud* to be with me! He was using his words to bring out the best in me.

In all those years I never dreamed that he might have rather made that trip alone (only recently did this occur to me). He never made me or my siblings feel that we were an inconvenience or a nuisance. He made me feel like he loved being with me, and by the look in his eye, I think he really did! That is what I want to give to my children. I want them to know that I am proud to be their mom and that I love being with them.

Recently I ran into a friend that I hadn't seen in a while and her daughters. I was telling them about our son's first summer camp experience and how I had missed him and longed for him to be home after his second day away. It was obvious I had missed him much more than he had missed me. Anyway, she laughingly made the comment, "You *still* miss yours, and I can't *wait* for mine to leave for college." I caught a glimpse of her older daughter rolling her eyes at her mom's cutting statement. Not knowing how to respond, she just looked away. . . . She was *not* laughing.

As I left that day, my heart hurt. I wasn't sure why I was so bothered by her statement. *It is very normal,* I thought, *for parents to feel frustrated with teenagers and even to look forward to their leaving.* I know that there will probably come a day when I will be more than ready for mine to leave too! I'm not denying the fact that those feelings are there for many parents, but I guess I believe you don't have to say everything you think, *especially* when your kids are standing right there. Our words are powerful to *build up* or to *tear down.* If we make our kids feel like they are not accepted by us, then we shouldn't be surprised when they seek to be accepted somewhere else.

Sharon and I have been blessed with an incredible mom. Not only was she amazingly efficient, she was also unbelievably wise. She knew the power of positive words in our lives and practiced them often. It would be in the midst of a mundane task that, out of the blue, Mom would wrap her arms around us and say something like, "You guys are so much fun; I can't imagine life getting any better. I think this stage in your life has to be the best."

The interesting thing was that she would tell us the same thing at every stage of our lives, even during those turbulent teen years. She may have been lying, but we believed her! Call it positive brainwashing or whatever you want, but it worked. We believed she loved and enjoyed being with us right where we were. And by talking about it, she believed it too.

"Every child should feel that there is no greater champion for his causes than his mother. The best person to confide in, to receive sympathy and affirmation from, should be the mom who gave the child life."[1]

Our kids need to know that we are their number one cheerleader! During the summer Olympics there was a story aired about Joan Read, a mom of one of the members of the U.S. rowing team. She had a bell that she would always ring in support of her son and his team as they streamlined through the water. On the show that day they asked to see her hands. When she turned them over, everyone could see that she had blisters from ringing the bell so much. What a wholehearted supporter![2] Our children are going to have plenty of people along the way willing to discourage them, so we as their moms need to build them up. Nan, a mom of a special-needs kid, tells her story:

> Be your child's advocate. Be willing to stand up for your child. The day after my son was born, I was obviously traumatized, but on top of that my grandmother passed away that day as well. A nurse came in, sat down, and said, "So, how many other retarded people do you have in your family?" At the time I didn't have the knowledge or strength to stand up for myself, but today I do! I encourage moms who have special-needs kids to have the courage to *stand up, speak out,* and *talk back.* One of my favorite names for Christ is "Advocate." I love that about my Lord. He stands in the gap for me and reminds me that "I can do all things through Christ who strengthens me."

encourage inner qualities not outward appearance

Another way our parents encouraged us was by complimenting our inner qualities. They did their best to focus on who God made us on the inside instead of always talking about outward qualities, such as looks, talents, and abilities. They wanted to make sure that we knew that God valued what was inside much more than what appeared on the outside.

Young and impressionable, I recall my father coming into the room while mom was fixing my hair. I would ask, "Daddy, do you like my hair?" He would answer, "I've got the prettiest girls in town!" But he would then follow with the question, "Are you just as pretty on the inside?" To which I would timidly answer "yes" and then jump into his arms and give him a big hug.

I try to do the same with my children. I will compliment them on their outward appearance (especially if they've worked really hard getting their hair just right), but will then ask, "Do you have a happy heart?" I always try to remind them that God cares so much more about who we are on the inside than what we look like on the outside.

First Samuel 16:7 assures us that this is God's focus too: "But the Lord said to Samuel, 'Do not consider his appearance or his height, for I have rejected him. The Lord does not look at the things man looks at. Man looks at the outward appearance, but the Lord looks at the heart.'"

Here are some suggestions on how to use your words to encourage your children's inner qualities: "You are . . . compassionate, caring, loving, kind, gentle, persistent, full of grace, forgiving, patient, unselfish, good at sharing, content, happy." You get the idea!

stop, drop, and restore your soul

I long for my words to represent my true feelings and desires for my kids. But in all the correcting and training we have to do as moms, our words may do just the opposite. And over the course of a "bad" day, our children may not *really* believe that we are proud of them. When we feel defeated because of our words with our children, it's good to stop, evaluate, and start over again.

1. What can you do to become a "yes" mom instead of a "no" mom?
2. How do you usually introduce your children to someone they've never met before?
3. Does it show them that you are proud of them and love being their mom?
4. Can you think of positive traits that are unique to your child that you could use when you introduce him or her?
5. What are some things you need to let go of and stop nagging your children about? Can you turn them over to God and let Him carry your burden?

Lord,

I feel so out of control at times with my children, and I end up saying things to them I don't really mean and wish I had never said. Forgive me for my unkind, undeserved words. I need help to be in Your control instead of out of control. Father, help me to think before I speak and to know when to back off and let You convict and discipline my children.

Thank You for my children, Lord. They are so precious to me. Help my words affirm and encourage them, not tear them down. I know You have a plan and a purpose for loaning them to me. Help me to trust You to bring Your plan to pass. Increase my confidence in You! Thank You, Lord. Amen.

making the most of the moments

1. **compliment café** At dinner ask each person to tell one thing they like or appreciate about every other member of the family. It

helps siblings and parents to verbalize the positive things they see.

2. **hide-a-note** When a family member is going on a trip (business trip, camp, to a friend's house) write notes of encouragement to the one who is leaving. Hide the notes throughout their bag. When your kids are old enough, get them involved (even if they can't write, they can draw a picture). My kids love hiding their notes in socks, pockets, and other fun places. Our mom did this with us when we were kids, and instead of being jealous that our sibling was getting to go somewhere we were not, we were excited for them to find all the surprises we'd hidden in their suitcase!

3. **God's gift** When you put a bow in your daughter's hair, tell her she is God's gift to you. Ask her if she is as pretty on the inside as she is on the outside.

chapter thirteen

being content with the unexpected

When Life Throws You a Curve

God has shown me that when I relax and let my life go the way God has planned it, I end up being much happier and more content. When I try to control things, nothing ends up working out.

Kathi

Trust in the Lord with all your heart and lean not on your own understanding; in all your ways acknowledge him, and he will make your paths straight.

(PROVERBS 3:5–6)

Not long ago I (Laurie) notified my husband, "I'm late," to which he replied, "Late for what?" In a whispered panic, I said, "I'm late! I haven't started—I may be pregnant!" He assured me that it was too early to jump to conclusions. He did not seem worried despite the fact that we were not trying or planning to have any more children. As a matter of fact, we were doing our best to prevent it. We already had three wonderful kids and only three bunks on our bus. I thought to myself, *Maybe he's right; I've been late before and it was a false alarm.*

I waited a few more days and there was no sign that Aunt Flow was gonna pay me a visit. Finally I couldn't stand to wait any longer and I told him, "I've got to buy a pregnancy test so that I can stop worrying."

As I drove to Wal-Mart that night with my nine-year-old son to buy last-minute items for his first summer camp, I had butterflies the whole way. I just couldn't stop thinking about the fact that I might be pregnant.

After finding all of his things, I encouraged him to go look at the toy aisle (which was close by) while I looked for a cheap, accurate, use-any-time-of-the-day pregnancy test. When I found one, I hid it under the new shorts I was buying so no one would see what I had.

We got home, showed Dad all the new stuff we'd purchased for camp, and then sent an excited young boy off to bed. It was late and he went to sleep right away.

I quickly grabbed the bag with the test in it and slipped off to the bathroom. I tore it open, my heart pounding. The instructions said it was 99 percent accurate any time of day. I read, "Positive results may appear as early as sixty seconds. However, wait at least three minutes after to be sure." The butterflies were doing flips in my stomach at this point. I tried to be optimistic and think that all the butterflies were about to fly away as soon as the test was done. I was sure that it was going to be negative.

I followed the instructions on the test and nervously sat it on the counter to watch and wait the three long minutes. My eyes began to water as I glared at the results. After only a few seconds lines began to appear everywhere. I was in shock. I kept looking at it and reading the instructions to make sure I was seeing it right. It was *positive*. What were we going to do?

About that time Charles walked in and said, "Can I be a part of this?" I began to sob: "I'm pregnant, honey! What are we going to do?" He wrapped his arms around me and said, "We're going to have another baby!" I blubbered: "I know, but where are we going to put it? We only have three bunks on our bus. Where will I have it—somewhere in another state? What's it going to do to our tour schedule? I'm thirty-eight years old, and we don't have any insurance! How could we be so irresponsible?" He just held me as I cried. The reality of it all was almost too much to deal with at that moment. It was late and I was exhausted. We finally went to bed, but I didn't sleep very well that night.

the fearful secret

The next day I awakened with the new knowledge looming over me like a black cloud. I called the doctor from the secrecy of my closet so the kids wouldn't hear. That's all I needed—for them to find out and go spreading the "good news of great joy" to friends and family.

I couldn't bear to think what people were going to say. I could already hear the comments: "Don't you know what causes that? Cooped up in that bus too much, huh? I thought you guys were all done." I cried just thinking about it. The nurse made an appointment for several weeks away. I wondered how I could keep this a secret for so long. Still, we had decided that we wouldn't tell anyone until after we returned home from Alec's week of camp. I would just have to keep the deep, dark secret.

Containing the "news" was difficult. The secret seemed so big to me that even though I hadn't talked to anyone about being pregnant, I was just sure those around me could feel the "baby vibes." Even so, I didn't tell anyone. Since I *had* to talk to someone, I started carrying on long conversations with myself and God. I thought, *If those women in the olden days could have babies in the back of a covered wagon, then surely I can go to the comforts of an unfamiliar hospital in another state and have a baby. You know, Laurie, it could be much worse.* I also thought, *The baby is going to be little and won't need much space on the bus, so we'll be able to manage for the few months we'll be on the road after it is born.*

I was trying hard not to think about the reality of my situation—until my sweet husband asked me to come look at something in the bus with him. I followed him out and was shocked when he began to describe ways he could overhaul the interior to accommodate our new addition. He had already been thinking of ways he could tear out our bed from the back of the bus and put four bunks in that space, putting our bed where the three stacked bunks had been, with some kind of fold-out bed thing.

I was already about to have a nervous breakdown on my own over the whole unexpected situation, and he was making it worse. I finally exclaimed, "Maybe we just need to sleep in separate bunks so we won't be in this predicament again!" He was stressing me out talking about all the renovations, so I reminded him, "The baby will only be about three months old by the time we are back home for the summer. Any changes can be made then; we don't have to even talk about this now!" How I longed for another woman to talk with, someone who would empathize and understand my shock and panic (no offense, honey). All week I felt like there was this huge balloon about to burst inside of me, but I did my best not to let one little bit of air leak out.

The time had come for us to take Alec to camp, and we were going to get to spend the week away at a resort nearby, thanks to the kindness of in-laws. I had managed to keep my secret safe and secure for seven whole days. I was thrilled we were going to have a whole week away from home because I wouldn't have to see people I knew and worry about accidentally leaking the news.

During the week away Charles took our girls to the pool each morning so that I would have time to write. I would try to concentrate on my writing but would always end up with my mind replaying all the questions I had about how we were going to deal with a new baby and the reality of all that was going to change in our lives. In my mind the challenges of the pregnancy were piling higher than I could see over, even standing on my tiptoes. Needless to say, I didn't get a whole lot accomplished on the book that week; my mind was too preoccupied.

During those days I found myself arguing with God, questioning this "blessing" He'd sent to us. Several nights I couldn't go to sleep. The uncertainties of my situation seemed to be constantly churning in my head. The more I focused on the questions, the bigger they grew. I couldn't seem to turn them off. One night through my tears, I asked God to help me stop worrying so I could sleep. He not only gave me rest but also assured me of His presence. He reminded me that He was in control.

He meets us where we are

God is faithful to meet us right where we are. He doesn't say, "I'll help you when you shape up and stop whining!" No, He just gently holds us right where we are while we work through our expectations and emotions, waiting for us to rest in Him. In 1 Peter 5:7 it says, "Cast all your anxiety on him because he cares for you."

By the end of the week my heart was beginning to soften. God tenderly reminded me that He was the creator of life (even though we sometimes think we are), and that He had a plan already in place for this new baby—and it *wasn't* to *wreck* our lives! It was like He was asking me, "Do you really believe what you talk about all the time—that children are a blessing, not a burden or an inconvenience?"

I could see that I wasn't trusting *His* plan for my life. I was throwing a tantrum instead. It was as if I were telling God that I could be content and happy as long as nothing unexpected happened in my life. When it did, I flew into a panic. I thought *I* knew what was best for my life and was convinced that having another baby right now wasn't the best!

Even amid all the shock and fear I was experiencing, there was a part of me that was a bit excited with the thought of being a mom again. When I would pass the baby things at the store, my heart would beat a little faster at the thought of doing the "baby thing" again. In my head I knew that God could be trusted with my life. I had trusted Him many times before and He had always been faithful. I knew that somehow it was all going to be okay. I finally began to let go of all the questions and gave them to God instead of worrying about them . . . knowing that He could handle them.

My friend Jennifer, who has a special-needs child, told me, "You know, what we think is the problem is really not the problem. The problem is not allowing God to handle the problem." How true that is. When I began to release my hold on my fears, God replaced them with His peace. I loved this little note I recently found. It is written as if it were from God, *"Good Morning! This is your heavenly Father—I will be handling all of your problems today. I will not need your help—so have a good day."*

After undergoing a week of intensive therapy with God, He felt I was ready to meet a kindred spirit, a real person I could talk with. The last day at the resort I was at the pool with the kids. A woman came and sat in the baby pool with her little boy. I was sitting there with Avery, my three-year-old daughter.

We began chitchatting about general topics, family, where we live, why we were there, etc., but quickly dove into the "deep end" of conversation, finding that we had many common interests and values. As I shared about our family traveling nine months out of the year in two big buses she became inquisitive. We suddenly realized we had a common passion for moms and families. She was a stay-at-home mom with a ministry to women, a writer, and a mother of four!

Even though she had a love for writing, she shared that her primary job was to be a mom—a woman after my own heart! Plus, she had *four* kids. *Four kids,* I thought. *Boy, do we ever have a lot in common. If she can do it, surely I can too.* As we shared our hearts with one another it wasn't long till we felt like we'd known each other forever. Our hearts were joined not only by a common bond as moms but also the common bond of Christ. She shared that she sent out a monthly e-devotional to women across the country, and I wanted to make sure I was on her e-list.

Before leaving the pool that day I shared with Dana our "big secret"—our unexpected baby who would become our fourth child. It felt so wonderful being able to tell someone out loud. And after telling her, I felt almost giddy inside. I figured she was safe to tell since I'd probably never see her again. She shared with me that her fourth child had been such a joy. She said, "I can't imagine life without him." She hugged me and encouraged me not to worry, saying, "God is going to work it all out. He has a plan for this child."

God has a plan

As I thought of God having a plan for this unexpected life in me, I thought of my friend Sue who told me that she had been an unexpected baby forty-something years ago. When her mom found out she was pregnant with her, she was very upset and tried to miscarry by jumping off the back porch! My heart sank when I heard her story. What would life have been like without Sue's passionate, enthusiastic personality? I'm so glad God's plan prevailed and her mom's didn't, because Sue has been such an incredible inspiration in my life and the lives of so many others. Again I was reminded that God does have a plan . . . I just have to trust Him!

As the girls and I walked away from the pool that day my burden was lighter. I thanked God for His remarkable love and grace in my life. I no longer had to bear the burden alone. I wanted to shout, "I'm going to have a baby, and it's going to be okay because God has a plan!" Now I *couldn't wait* to tell the "good news of great joy" about this unexpected pregnancy. God was helping me become content even in a situation that wasn't expected. I was going to get to be a mom . . . and loving it . . . *again*!

stop, drop, and restore your soul

As I was thinking about my unexpected pregnancy I reflected upon two of the most remarkable "unexpected pregnancies" in history. I found it interesting that both of the pregnant women spoken of in Luke 1 were unlikely candidates for motherhood. One was very old and one was very young (and unwed). But both, when confronted with God's announcement of their unexpected pregnancy, accepted and embraced His call on their lives. If anyone had the right to be angry at God, and ask Him, "Why now?" they did.

Elizabeth could have shouted, "God, You've got to be kidding! I'm so old that I won't be able to keep up with a baby. If You can make this happen *now*, why didn't You do it years ago when we were younger and cried out to You?"

And Mary ... well, she probably had even more reason to throw a fit about her "unplanned" pregnancy. Her whole life was going to change. She was engaged to a man but not yet married, and now she was going to be pregnant ... but not with *his* child. How was she going to explain this one? She could very likely be publicly disgraced, maybe even stoned to death!

These two stories bring hope and encouragement to me: Hope in the understanding that God has a plan and a purpose, and He is going to get us through our current circumstances even when we don't understand them, and encouragement that sometimes God manifests himself most gloriously in the lives of people who experience the unexpected. Think of what came from these two unlikely women—two sons whose lives changed the course of *all* mankind. These were two ordinary moms who were called to mother the extraordinary. Wow! Don't underestimate God's plan for your life, even when it doesn't make sense to you.

1. What have you been whining or complaining about during the past few days or weeks that doesn't seem fair, or doesn't make sense to you (a move, job change, layoff, singleness)?
2. Are you fighting and arguing with God about where you are right now? How can you rest in His plan even when it isn't what you expected?
3. What is keeping you from trusting God in your situation? What is your greatest fear regarding the circumstances you're in?

Dear Lord,
I am scared and feel out of control. Help me trust You in my situation.

Help me in my unbelief. Take away the fear that I'm experiencing and replace it with the peace that only You can give. Help me rest in You as I walk through these challenging, unpredictable times, knowing You will never leave me or forsake me. I know that I am Your child. You love me and care for me more than I could ever love and care for my children. Thank You for Your love. I pray in the name of Your precious Son, whom You gave for me. Amen.

making the most of the moments

1. **"a child is born"** Read Luke 1 and try putting yourself in the shoes of these two unlikely moms. Observe their response to the "unexpected" and write down key words that describe their reactions.
2. **the good, the bad, and the ugly** Write a letter or write in a journal how you are feeling right where you are. Express your feelings … the good, bad, and the ugly! Don't hold back. God knows right where you are, and He loves you. You can tell Him what you are feeling.
3. **faith reminders** Make a list of God's faithfulness to you in the past. Read over the list when you need to be reminded that God is in control and has a plan for your life.
4. **share your burdens** Find a friend with whom you can be honest. Share your current struggle. Ask her to pray with and for you during this unexpected situation.
5. **trusting Him** Memorize Proverbs 3:5–6 and post it in a place where you can see it throughout the day.

chapter fourteen

being content with life
When It Doesn't Make Sense

My son has a cyst in his brain that grew since birth. We did not find it until he was five years old. God has taught me I cannot control things, hard as I might try. He has taught me that my children are His and I am guiding them, but they could be called home from me at any time.
Christine

And the peace of God, which transcends all understanding, will guard your hearts and your minds in Christ Jesus.

(PHILIPPIANS 4:7)

It was finally time to spread the news about baby number four! After telling some of my close friends, they decided to come and secretly decorate all our vehicles with the wonderful news (even our forty-foot bus—thanks for your support and shoe polish, Dana, Sandy, and Dinina). There was no keeping it a secret any longer; the word was out.

As I began to accept and rest in God's unexpected plan for our lives, the pieces of the puzzle began to fall into place. For example, the due date was at a time when we were already going to be home for Christmas. This meant we were able to extend our break a little to allow time for me and the baby to recuperate before heading back out for our spring tour.

Financially, God had provided through an unforeseen means (and to be quite honest, very humbling) to help pay the cost of our medical bills. I was eligible for Medicaid through a program for pregnant moms. At first I was horrified, humiliated, and resentful about the whole idea. *I can't believe I'm having to get help from the state,* I thought piously to myself.

I used to be the one who was going with other people to get help, when I was a social worker.

Each time I went to the Department of Human Services I would pray that I wouldn't see someone I used to work with, or knew. I was embarrassed. In my mind I could hear them remarking, "Oh, your ministry must be going really well if you're eligible for Medicaid." I wondered, "God, if we *are* doing what You called us to do, shouldn't we be able to pay for this baby?" However, as time passed, I became *very thankful* for the financial assistance God had provided through the state of Texas.

I was about ten and a half weeks along when we finally had our first doctor's appointment. Charles went with me and helped me fill out the preliminary paper work that took almost two hours. We were given all the new baby literature, as well as a bag full of samples and other freebees. We talked with the nurse practitioner, Rose, about our surprise and excitement as she shared about unexpected surprises in her life. She assured us that God was in control and had a plan.

As our two-hour appointment came to a close, it was finally time to take a peek at our little miracle in progress. It was time for the sonogram. As Rose moved the wand back and forth, I spotted a glimpse of the baby. Finally she was able to get a good angle, settling on the tiny figure in my womb. Our eyes were fixed on the screen as we looked at the helpless form.

Then it was as if time began to move in slow motion for me. My heart began to pound in my chest, and I blurted out in a pleading voice, hoping somebody would prove me wrong, "I don't see a heartbeat . . . there is no heartbeat!" Straining to see beyond what she could make out, Rose sadly agreed. "I don't either, Laurie." She kept searching as I began to weep.

I felt as if we had been running in one direction, momentum building, when all of a sudden a brick wall had been abruptly thrown up in front of us—one we didn't see until we ran, full throttle, into it. We could go no further in that direction. Suddenly we were left with nothing more than vacant hopes and dreams; everything had been snatched away in an instant. All we could do was walk away, empty-handed.

Wiping tears from my eyes, I despondently laid all the "mommy materials" I had been given only moments before on the counter and walked out of the room in a daze. This was the end of this chapter in my life . . . and it had only just begun.

Immediately we were ushered to another room to fill out necessary paper work for the hospital where the "procedure" was scheduled for early the following morning. I felt like I was going to throw up. *How could this be? Surely this is only a bad dream. We were just expecting a baby, and now we're not!* I felt as if I were walking around in a fog; my thoughts were a jumble. *This was supposed to be a happy day. I've been waiting for it for weeks. Just when I finally came to accept and get excited about this baby, it's gone. God, this doesn't make any sense!*

when the bottom falls out

The days that followed were filled with tears, bewilderment, disorientation, fear, and constant questioning. I felt the need to talk about what had happened, but could hardly find the energy to return the overwhelming number of phone calls from concerned friends. I replayed the whole experience in my mind, questioning God's purpose in it all. The only peace from the nagging reality came through sleep, and that didn't always come easily.

When I would awaken, the gloom would settle in again. I was unmotivated and apathetic about my responsibilities. But because I had three children who still needed a functioning mother, I had to continue on. There were things I knew I needed to do, but I couldn't find the strength to accomplish the task. I needed to work on this book, because our deadline was approaching. But for two whole weeks I didn't write one word and had no desire to do so.

There were days I felt as if I were in a bubble, watching the world go on without me. I was truly "in the world, but not of it." I found myself resenting the fact that others could just "go on" as though nothing was wrong. I didn't want to be alone, and yet I didn't want to be with people. Some words of encouragement were truly comforting and others were hurtful. I kept thinking, *If I can just talk about it enough, I think I can make sense of it all.*

But no matter how much I talked, it never seemed to make any sense. My mind couldn't comprehend or assimilate all the questions and thoughts I had floating around in my head. Dr. James Dobson, in his book *When God Doesn't Make Sense*, states, "Many of our questions—especially those that begin with the word *why*—will have to remain unanswered for the time being."[1]

During my time of grief, I needed my husband far more than he seemed to need me. I constantly wanted to be near him, to have him hold me and let me cry. *He should feel the same way I'm feeling,* I thought. *He lost a child too.* And yet he wasn't grieving like I was. We were two different people, grieving two different ways. He cried, but then he was able to move on with life rather quickly. I, on the other hand, simply wanted life to stop and acknowledge that I had lost my baby!

I also wondered, "Why did God bother to work out all the details for this child to enter our lives if He knew it would never be born?" I questioned God: "Why did I have to experience the whole Medicaid ordeal if I wasn't going to have this baby? It wasn't very pleasant, and I was made to feel like a nobody." However, looking back at the whole financial situation, I can see that God's provision through the state of Texas relieved the burden of the medical expenses that were incurred during our loss. Many families who experience the tragedy of miscarriage are faced with not only the loss of a baby but also the accumulated medical expenses. Each month they send in a payment to the hospital it is an awful reminder that they are paying for a baby they never got to hold.

Through all my contemplation during this painful time in my life, I did come to a few humble thoughts about it all.

- First, I don't think God *caused* this to happen to me. He may have *allowed* it, but He didn't *cause* it.

- Second, it didn't happen because I had done something to deserve it.

- Third, He didn't *choose* me to be the one to go through this pain and struggle because I was stronger than others or more spiritual and could therefore "handle it."

- And finally, He didn't pick me to go through this experience *simply* so that I would have a story to share in our ministry.

nothing is wasted

Even though I don't believe God specifically *chose* me for this trial so I would be able to use it in our ministry, I do believe that He can and will use difficulties in my life, as well as yours, to bring about something good—if we will let Him. God is able to take all the broken pieces of our lives and miraculously put them together to accomplish His purposes and plans.

Romans 8:28 is so encouraging to me: "And we know that in *all* things God works for the good of those who love him, who have been called according to his purpose" (emphasis added). It doesn't say "only when good things happen" can He carry out His "good" in our lives. It says "in all things" (to me that means the good times, the bad times, and the ugly times) "God works for the good of those who love him." So many times we feel that God is against us and is causing bad things to happen to us when the reality is, *He is on our side*—constantly loving us and working in and through our situations to bring about good in our lives. He loves us. Our circumstances don't limit God's ability to accomplish the good He has planned for us.

I have found that one of the "good" things that can come from difficult circumstances in our lives is that (in time) we can comfort someone else who is hurting. 2 Corinthians 1:3 says, "Praise be to the God and Father of our Lord Jesus Christ, the Father of compassion and the God of all comfort, who *comforts us in all our troubles, so that we can comfort those in any trouble* with the comfort we ourselves have received from God" (emphasis added). Notice it says, He "comforts us so we can comfort others." It doesn't say He brings trials so we can comfort others. Trials are inevitable, but it is God's comfort that brings good out of them.

When the news got out of my miscarriage, I was flooded with cards and calls from concerned friends. Many of the cards I received were from women who had also experienced the heartbreak of miscarriage. For some it had been thirty years ago. I had never known it about them. These women were able to comfort me with great sensitivity and understanding, describing my emotions precisely, because they had been through it.

My friend Stacia, who delivered her baby girl on Mother's Day in her fifth month of pregnancy, comforted me when she shared,

> In the beginning, the tears would come as soon as I opened my eyes each morning. The tears and void are normal, and part of our grieving process. There were times that I could discuss every

moment of loss without hesitation, and then others when I would see a little girl in a carrier and lose it. Although we will never forget, with time it gets easier. We literally felt Philippians 4:7 come to life: "And the peace of God, which passeth all understanding, shall keep your hearts and minds through Christ Jesus" (KJV). I am praying this for you and every member of your family.

Another e-mail I received was from a friend in Arizona. Because she had also experienced the loss of a baby, she was able to provide comfort to me through her own story.

We delivered our three-pound baby girl on May 4. The doctors were unable to give me a confirmed reason why she died. She was perfectly healthy. We have had a tremendous outpouring of comfort and support from family and friends but we still miss our baby. I wish I could just sit and talk and pray with you. I do understand. God loves you. He loves you so much. My heart aches with yours. Find comfort in knowing our babies are rejoicing with our Father and our Lord Jesus. In His love, Heather.

Because we live in a fallen world it is a fact that bad things happen—things that may never make any sense to us. But be assured that God has not forsaken you. Isaiah 41:10 says, "Do not fear, for I am with you; do not be dismayed, for I am your God. I will strengthen you and help you; I will uphold you with my righteous right hand." He's waiting to hold you up when you don't have the strength to stand . . . just let Him.

embrace your grief

Women can experience loss in many different ways. You may be grieving because of a miscarriage, the loss of a loved one, a recent divorce, an abortion, a special-needs child, or the loss of your own childhood. Your life has been changed forever, leaving a void that seems to consume you at times. You wonder if you'll ever be able to "go on" with your life again. Some days you don't even want to.

Maybe you've experienced the heartbreak of miscarriage like me. You may feel your grief isn't as real as someone else's because you never had a baby to hold. You may think, "How can I grieve this deeply over someone I never knew?" But just the same, your life has suddenly taken a turn that doesn't make any sense. No matter the circumstances of the loss of your loved one, the brick wall of this shocking death has stopped you in your tracks and forced you down a path of grief you never intended to go.

Perhaps you are grieving the loss of a long and happy marriage or a short-lived one. You have had to lay down your bag of hopes and dreams and walk away empty-handed because of an unwanted divorce or an unexpected death. You may be thinking, *I never imagined that my life would turn out this way—I didn't want to be a single mom.* You find yourself grieving for your children as well: "Why do they have to grow up in a single-parent home?" One single mom said, "I knew it didn't make sense, but shortly after my husband's death, I found myself being angry at *him* for leaving me with two small children." The hurt can be so deep for a single mom that she doesn't know how she'll ever rise above it.

Or perhaps you've experienced loss through an abortion. You may feel that you don't have the right to grieve because of the choices you've made. And yet your heart aches with pain and guilt. You may have realized at some point that you needed to grieve, but you didn't feel you had permission to talk about your loss with anyone. You thought if you didn't talk about it the feelings would go away . . . but they linger like a dark cloud hovering over you. The guilt is sometimes more than you can bear. And even though you know God can forgive you—1 John 1:9 assures us of this—you can't seem to forgive yourself. (For help, see Post-Abortion Support Services in Appendix one.)

You may be a mom with a special-needs child. You find yourself repeatedly grieving what your child will never be. You have had to put away preconceived expectations of your child and adjust to new ones. You grapple with trying to understand "why." Contentment is, many times, hard to find.

Perhaps you are mourning the loss of your own childhood because of abuse, death of a parent, alcohol, or divorce. You worry about how you will be able to provide your children with a wholesome childhood when you don't know what one is. You want to break the negative cycle in your life but don't know how.

For those of you in the midst of grief you may be experiencing a myriad of emotions—everything from denial, bargaining, anger, and depression to forgiveness and acceptance. You may face one or all of the emotions on any given day. Grief is unpredictable and many times illogical. Grief comes in many shapes and forms. Unfortunately, it is not packaged nice and neat, handed to you to be opened, with the gift of sudden healing inside.

One day you may feel like you are through the grieving process; you think, *I haven't cried in several days, I must be doing better; maybe I'm all done with this and can move on now.* The trouble is, the very next day you are hit with a wave of overwhelming depression and sadness. Emotions run crazy in the midst of grief, but they are normal.

Job, in the Bible, went through tremendous heartache and loss. He didn't hold back his feelings or emotions but cried out to God in the midst of his pain: "I have no peace, no quietness; I have no rest, but only turmoil" (Job 3:26), and again in chapter 6:2–3: "If only my anguish could be weighed and all my misery be placed on the scales! It would surely outweigh the sand of the seas." Wow, he didn't have trouble putting his feelings into words!

So don't be afraid to express your thoughts and feelings to God. He already knows what they are. Talk to Him, cry out to Him, ask Him, "Why?"—you can even scream at Him. He loves you and is near even when you don't feel Him. Grief must *not* be avoided. It cannot be rushed, dodged, buried, or escaped. Grief is a necessity. As Michele Howe says, "Grieving is not wasted time, it's growing time."[2]

If you have experienced a loss in your life, but have never allowed yourself to grieve, and instead have stuffed your feelings, don't simply assume you are "over it." Larry Yeagley, in his book *Grief Recovery,* states, "In grief, pain is a sign of healing. Feeling and expressing pain is healthy and absolutely essential."[3] Grief will reveal itself in one way or another.

Many times unresolved grief manifests itself through these symptoms: chronic illness, repeated criminal activity, self-destructive behavior (eating disorders, drugs, alcohol), multiple relationships, abusive behavior (physical, verbal, sexual, emotional), bad choices, chaotic homelife, anger, bitterness, and unforgiveness. If you are experiencing some of these symptoms, look carefully at the losses in your life. Determine whether or not you have allowed yourself to grieve. If you are still struggling, seek help through Christian counseling, support groups, and/or grief-related resources. We have listed a few resources in Appendix one for those traveling this difficult road.

grieving with hope

Two days after our loss Alec, my ten-year-old son, fell on his bed in a heap of tears. Lying down beside him, we cried together. He looked at me and asked, "How long will we feel like this?" I told him, "It won't hurt this bad forever. Each day the times that we feel sad and cry will become less and less." I encouraged him to just feel whatever he was feeling; if he was mad or angry, I told him it was okay to feel that way. If he was sad and wanted to cry, then that was what he needed to do.

Nothing can take away the grief process. You must walk through it one step at a time. Be patient with yourself. We all grieve in different ways, and the time it takes is unique to each person.

As Christians we sometimes equate spiritual depth with one's ability to "be strong" after a loss in their life. We might believe that the stronger someone is (i.e., not crying or showing emotion) the more spiritual that person must be. In 1 Thessalonians 4:13 it says not to "grieve like the rest of men, who have no hope." As Christians, it does not say we are *not* to grieve; it's just that we should not grieve as those who have no *hope*.

During my time of grief, people would come to me and ask, "How are you doing?" I would try to answer the ones that I felt *really* wanted to know by saying, "I'm still hurting, but not without hope!" That's healthy grief. Grieving has nothing to do with the strength or weakness of our faith. It has everything to do with our humanity. It is normal and healthy to grieve, and abnormal and unhealthy not to.

When I was in college I memorized all of Psalm 139. I have repeated the words many times through the years, and it has always brought comfort to me. However, rereading it during my time of loss provided new meaning in my life. The particular day I was reading it I felt like a dark, dense fog was hovering over me and it just wouldn't go away. Then I read these words (Psalm 139:11–12): "If I say, 'Surely the darkness will hide me and the light become night around me,' even the darkness will not be dark to you; the night will shine like the day, for darkness is as light to you."

This brought renewed hope to me, the fact that even though darkness felt like it was going to consume me, it could not consume God. He would eventually make my "night shine like the day." As we were riding in the car about a week after my miscarriage, Abby, my seven-year-old, stated, "Mommy, it seems like when we were going to have a baby our days were brighter." I agreed with her, but assured her that God was going to help our days become "bright" again—He promised!

stop, drop, and restore your soul

This chapter may have taken you by surprise; its contents may have been totally unexpected. You may be asking, "Okay, what does grief have to do with being a mom and loving it? I thought this book was about finding contentment in real life!" Unfortunately, loss and suffering are a part of real life. That's why we wrote this chapter.

Maybe you saw the direction of this chapter and were tempted to jump to the next chapter. I'm glad you didn't. Whether you've ever experienced grief or not, you will be able to better understand those who have by reading about it. Let God soften your heart toward those who are going through difficult times. You never know how God will use you to show His love and comfort to someone who needs it.

Perhaps you are right in the middle of grief, experiencing many of the emotions described. You know firsthand the agony of pain. My heart aches with you. If I could take the pain away, I would. But that isn't the way it works. I don't want to sound like I'm uttering clichés, but I've found that time really does heal the heart.

I encourage you to give yourself that time. Talk to friends about your loss as many times as you need to. Keep a journal of your thoughts and feelings. Someday you'll be able to pick it up and see that you really are growing through your grief. Read books about grief. When you're ready, read the Psalms. No matter what you are feeling, always keep an open line of communication with God. Tell Him what you're feeling. He already knows, and He loves you unconditionally.

1. What losses have you experienced in your life? What evidence do you see that indicates you have grieved through your losses? If you haven't allowed yourself to do so, what is keeping you from grieving? (busyness, disbelief, "spirituality," too strong to cry?)

2. If you are in the midst of grieving a loss, what emotions are

you currently experiencing? How long have you been where you are? When do you think it is necessary to get additional help to work through the grieving process?

3. If you have passed through the grieving process, how have you seen God at work throughout? How might He use your experience to encourage or help someone else?

4. What have you done to help a friend who has experienced a loss? How will you be more sensitive to someone who has experienced a loss after reading this chapter?

Father,

I know my situation has not caught You by surprise. As I cry tears for my loss, You cry tears for the pain that I am suffering. Heavenly Father, You are not unfamiliar with loss. You alone know where I am in this process of grieving. I take You by the hand and ask You to help me through the steps I need to take. I look forward to the day when my precious one welcomes me into heaven to meet You. Until then, I trust that You will guide me in finding contentment no matter what my circumstances might be. I look forward to seeing what good You will bring out of this loss as well as how You will use me and my situation to bless others. I praise You. Amen.

making the most of the moments

1. **take time** List the significant losses in your life. Do you feel that you have allowed yourself time to grieve these losses? If not, why not? Take time this week to think about each loss and see what emotions arise. Write in your journal about your experience.

2. **talk about it** Discuss with a friend whether or not you feel "stuck" in a particular stage of grief. Reflect on what might be holding you back. (Are you rushing yourself, or are you dwelling on particular issues of your loss that keep you from being able to forgive?) Do you feel it is time to move on? Write down the steps you're going to take to move out of your "stuck" state.

3. **forgive** Forgiveness is necessary for real healing. As you look at your loss, make a list of those people you may need to forgive.

In Luke 23:34, Christ gave us the perfect example of unmerited forgiveness. Read that verse as you pray over your list. Ask Him to help you apply the same forgiveness to each of the names you listed, even if you feel the hurt was intentional. Ask God to deliver you from the hurt they have caused.

4. **write** Keep a journal (always date your entries) of lessons learned through your grieving process. Look back from time to time to see how far you've come. God can use your situation to help others who may experience a similar loss. When you are ready, prepare your story to share with others.

5. **reach out** If you haven't personally experienced a loss mentioned in this chapter, think of a person who *has* and consider how you could be used to encourage or comfort that person. (Maybe you could just listen to them without any explanation or advice; fix them a meal; write a card or note to them, etc.) If you know someone who has traveled this road, ask that person what was most helpful to her at the time.

chapter **fifteen**

the gray-haired angels
Their Secret to Becoming a Mom and Loving It!

This life curriculum may not be what I would have chosen, but because it's what my Heavenly Father wants for me I accept it and embrace it. My natural ways lean toward comfort and ease, but His ways are higher than my ways. He knows what I need in the school of life to be conformed to the image of Christ. He also knows what my child needs in order to learn about the character and ways of God.

Linda

He tends his flock like a shepherd: He gathers the lambs in his arms and carries them close to his heart; he gently leads those that have young.

(ISAIAH 40:11)

Continued from chapter 1) As my little man got bigger we were on the go, a lot! I (Laurie) would take him everywhere with me; you know, I couldn't *just* stay at home. I was almost on a first-name basis with the clerks at Wal-Mart because we were there so much. I was determined that having a baby was not going to change my lifestyle or slow me down. I was going to go and do the things I'd always done.

But as I was doing all my running around, a curious thing kept happening. I would run into these interesting people—everywhere I went—that I called gray-haired angels. These were individuals I had never met who would come up to me, out of the blue, and start talking to my kids and me. I would look around to see if there was a sign somewhere pointing to me that said, "Desperate Mom . . . Needs Advice." Everywhere I went it kept happening!

The gray-haired angels would immediately begin admiring my baby, looking into his eyes and reaching for his little fingers to wrap around theirs. Being a new mom, I would panic, thinking "He's going to get some kind of awful germ . . . I wish they wouldn't touch his hands."

It was always the same. These sweet, well-meaning, gray-haired individuals would offer their free advice to the "new" mom, saying things like "Honey, you'd better enjoy him. It goes by in a hurry." I would graciously acknowledge what they were saying, and think, *I am enjoying him, but you must have forgotten how* hard *this is! I have no life! How am I supposed to enjoy that?* I was sure I would be changing diapers for the next eighteen years.

When we added another baby to our clan two and a half years later (just as things were getting a little easier), I was now *positive* that I would be changing diapers forever! I was back to square one. However, the phenomenon of the gray-haired angels continued. Each time I took the kids anywhere, complete strangers, with a twinkle in their eyes, would reminisce about their own children as they looked at mine and would offer the same "free" advice as all the others. "You'd better enjoy it . . . they'll be grown before you know it." Then they would say, "It seems like yesterday when mine were little, and now they are forty-five and fifty years old."

Again I would try to be gracious, but inside I wanted to scream, *Lady, I do enjoy them, but can't you see I'm struggling here, trying to keep these two kids in the grocery cart? They're crying, smushing my bread, ready for their nap, and hungry! And you say I'm supposed to find pleasure in this? You've got to be kidding! If you think they're so great, why don't you take one of them home with you?*

Sometimes the days would get very long. Money was short, and it was harder to get around with two kids and their nap schedules, so our trips to Wal-Mart were limited to "necessary" trips instead of "I need to get out of the house" trips. There were days when I was sure the walls were going to close in on me and I was going to lose my mind. The house was constantly a mess, with toys everywhere and clothes on the floor that had been thrown there by a child who had already changed three times by noon. I was weary of talking "baby talk" and longing for adult conversation. I was constantly "picking-up," but the messes would multiply faster than I could clean them up. I was ready for my kids to be out of the "demolition" stage. I was having a hard time enjoying the moments.

enjoy the moments?

As the responsibility of two children grew, so did my feelings of frustration, guilt, discontentment, and resentment. Often I would think *This isn't how I* planned *to feel about motherhood. Maybe I'm not cut out for this. What if I can't do this? Maybe I should just go back to work!*

One afternoon I was sitting on the floor holding Abby while Alec was playing beside us. I was in a "funk" again, and couldn't get out of it. I felt defeated and useless. "God, I know there must be something to what those gray-haired angels have been telling me, but I just can't see it. What is so wonderful about where I am right now? They say, 'Enjoy it while it lasts . . . it will go by in a hurry.' So why am I not enjoying it? What is wrong with me? This is where I've wanted to be all my life, and now that I'm here, all I can do is wish to be somewhere else."

As my eyes welled up with tears, I glanced down at the chubby hands in front of me. I noticed the little dimples, the ones where knuckles are supposed to be. I had seen them many times, but I hadn't *really seen* them. I thought to myself, *Their hands won't look or feel like this forever.* I gently rubbed my thumb across the dimples. That night, as I bathed my kids, I thought of a friend who would give anything to bathe a child again, to feel the soft skin of a baby, because she loves children but her children are grown. "I give them a bath every night but rarely think of it as a privilege," I realized.

Several days later I was walking with my girls, holding their hands. I had my three-year-old's squishy little hand in my left hand and my seven-year-old's slender hand in my right. That day I really *felt* them. (Usually I'm dragging them!) In that moment I thanked God for the hands He'd given me to hold.

I realized, in those instances, that God was allowing me to see the preciousness of my children right at the moment. He was changing my perspective right where I was. Nothing had changed in my situation. But my viewpoint was changing! I had a renewed glimmer of hope and purpose for my life.

"Enjoy the moments . . . they go by in a hurry!" I'll bet you've heard this from some gray-haired angels too! Sometimes we're in such a hurry, we miss the little squinty eyes saying "cheese" for another photo, chubby arms squeezing our neck, fingerprints on the glass door (remember, someday they won't be there to wipe off), the belly laugh of a child, smushed-nose good-night kisses, toys scattered on the floor, little hands reaching for ours, unexpectedly hearing, "Mom, I love you," and sneaking a hug from a preteen who still needs his mom's love.

The list could go on and on. Those little old ladies really know what they're talking about, don't they? Why is it that they have such a clear view of what is most important when we often don't? I can think of four possible reasons: As moms we are in survival mode; we have a hard time lightening up; we expect our kids to act like little adults; and we are longing for tomorrow.

survival mode

When we are in the midst of raising young children, life can overwhelm us, taking our focus off of what is most important. We can become so consumed by all the demands of our lives that we shift to "survival mode." We are not able to enjoy where we are in life because of life itself. The bills pile up, the laundry is overwhelming, the house is constantly a mess, the kids are sick and have to be taken to the doctor, husbands aren't home very much or don't help out when they are home (unless, of course, you remember to ask for help *before* you're angry), and to top it all off, as a mom, you feel you don't have a life anymore.

When we are simply *surviving* we don't have time for *living*. After a concert one night a mom with young children told me that she e-mailed her mother and her sister, recounting her busy week with her family. She reported on who had been to the doctor and why, who had played ball games, what she hadn't accomplished that she meant to, etc. Her sister responded to her e-mail with her own explanation of her past week, telling of all the activities they'd been involved in—who had dentist appointments, recitals, etc. She complained about how expensive it was to raise kids. Both sisters expressed feelings of being behind and feeling overwhelmed. In response, their mom e-mailed both her daughters and simply stated, "Today I got up, let the dog out, ate breakfast, and read the paper. Enjoy it! It goes by in a hurry."

We know that our children are what is most important, but the "stuff of life" causes us to forget. We become stressed with life, and, sadly, many times we take our stress out on our children.

My son told me one night before bed, "Mommy, I don't want you to stay up late again tonight." (He had heard me complaining about being tired earlier that day.) When I began explaining the reasons I had to stay up late (to fold clothes, wash the dinner dishes, pick up toys, etc.), he responded, "I'm sorry, Mommy." Then I felt horrible. It wasn't *his* fault I had so much to do. If we are not careful, we will make our children feel they are to blame for the responsibilities we carry.

It is a privilege to be a mom, but it is easy to miss that fact when we're bombarded with all the things that moms have to do and be. When I began noticing, and thanking God (out loud) for the little things in my life, my perspective changed. There were (and still are) days when I have to choose whether I will see my day as one to be *survived* or as one that I will *enjoy*.

Kelli, a mom of a two- and four-year-old, candidly shared:

When I look at moms who seemingly have it all—the great house, the amazing car (not the 1992 Toyota with 154,000 miles), the perfectly dressed kids, and the job that sounds too good to be true—it is often hard not to let that one thought cross your mind . . . *Now, what if I were . . .* and you fill in the blank (still working, married to someone else, blah, blah, blah). The "what ifs" are out there, even for the strongest of Christian women.

But, then I tuck those little babies into their beds at night and I look into their sleepy little eyes, and I hear that "I love you sooooo much, Mommy!" And I know once again that those other things just don't matter. I am already married to the best guy in the world, we live in a wonderful place just right for us at this time of our lives, I praise God that the wheels aren't falling off the car—and that we have no car payment! And that God has gifted me, absolutely GIFTED me with the most precious treasure He could offer—a child.

lighten up!

Because life is full of harsh realities and difficult circumstances, parents can become so serious that they lose the ability to "lighten up" and have fun. I (Laurie) remember a time in my childhood when my grandfather was keeping us (me, my older brother, and younger sister) while my mom (his daughter) was having surgery. We were giggling, like kids do, as we walked to his car. He was evidently worried about my mom and fussed at us for laughing and being silly, saying, "This isn't a time to be playing!"

I remember the three of us getting very quiet, and I began to worry that my mom must be really sick if granddad was that worried. Grandad didn't mean to be harsh, of course, but as adults it's hard for us at times to not allow our seriousness to spill over on our children. It is in those times that it is difficult to allow children to be children. Kids don't understand serious. That's not how they are wired. Their work is play and they need to be allowed to play.

One mom who was probably expecting too much from her girls said, "I just wanted them to get more done (homework, chores, straightening up), but I failed to realize their need to have a break or unstructured time . . . because playing is their job right now! Sometimes I forget how important it is for them just to play dolls together."

You have to *make yourself* lighten up; it doesn't come naturally for most adults. But it is vitally important in a child's life. My kids love it when their dad or mom acts silly or plays with them. Their eyes light up and big grins come across their faces. One day after visiting the library, we were walking to the car with an armful of books. I stopped on the lawn of the library, put the books down by the tree, and said, "Let's play tag! Alec, you're it!" He looked at me like I was crazy and then started chasing me. He loved it. It didn't take more than five minutes, but I made myself stop my "adult world" to do something I knew he loved to do.

"little adults"

We are so concerned with raising our children "right" and wanting them to do their best that our expectations can sometimes exceed their capabilities. Not only is it hard for us as parents to lighten up and play with our kids, but we expect our children to act like us. Children are only little for a short while. We need to let them *be kids*.

Many moms have e-mailed us saying they expected their children to act like "little adults." I sometimes think it comes out of our desire to make them behave properly, which is a noble goal as long as it is age-appropriate. I found my expectations to be especially high with our first child. I think as parents we don't know what to expect because they are the first, and we can be extra hard on them. We sometimes put responsibilities on them that they are not ready to bear, expecting them to be something they aren't ready to be.

Sarah, a mom with two young children, said, "One day my two-year-old decided to start swinging one of his little golf clubs around, trying to knock the pictures off the wall. I couldn't get to him, and yelled at my four-year-old to grab the golf club away from him. She responded by telling me, 'I'm not the parent!' Perspective gained."

Another mom told of a similar incident where she caught herself expecting her preschooler to act more like the parent than the child. She said,

> I stepped into the kitchen to grab something, leaving my three-year-old son with my nine-month-old daughter. When I returned to the room I realized my daughter had put something in her mouth. Once I got it out, I fussed at my three-year-old for not watching her. He came up to me and said, 'Mommy, I'm sorry. I didn't know she had anything.' I felt about two inches high. First, why did I ever expect him to be the caregiver? Second, why didn't I handle it better? I was crushed. (Ann)

Sarah and Ann aren't the only moms who've done this. We've all done it. There is extraordinary pressure from society to make your children "grow up" before they are ready. Just look at the little girls' clothes that look like clothes for teenagers, or the opportunity for young children to participate in activities that used to be reserved for older kids. Take a stand and allow your kids to be kids! Don't succumb to the pressure to "push" your kids into adulthood.

Another way we expect our kids to act like little adults is to schedule every moment of their time with structured activities. Some kids need their own Day-Timer by the young age of four to keep up with all their appointments! Don't get caught in this trap. There are a lot of "good" things available for our children to be involved in, but sometimes the best thing for them is to have unstructured playtime at home.

kid stuff

The reality is, "Kids will be kids," and fortunately kids *want* to be kids . . . so allow them to be. Here are some things that are common to most all children. If yours do any or all of these, they are in good company. You might as well laugh instead of cry about it!

- Kids sometimes run in public places when you don't want them to.
- Kids forget and talk with their mouths full.
- Kids are all about fairness . . . (though it will never be fair enough).
- Kids will get hurt over and over again.
- Kids love it when they bleed, if it doesn't hurt too bad.
- Kids are loud (no matter where you are).
- Kids will share private matters in public places.
- Kids are manipulative (they have much more time to scheme than you have time to avert their plans).
- Kids are forgiving.
- Kids, especially boys, love to talk about and demonstrate bodily functions (at the most inopportune times).
- Kids get into trouble.
- Kids pick their noses in public.
- Kids will embarrass you at times.
- Kids know how to push your buttons and set you up for a reaction.
- Kids wipe their dirty hands on their clean clothes and yours.

One frustrated mom felt a little silly after screaming at her daughter, "Why can't you act your age?" Then she realized she was—she was only three years old! It is so easy to forget how young our children are at times. We forget that they haven't been around long enough to learn it all yet.

Another mom shared what helped her to gain a proper perspective of her kids. She said, "Talking to friends and hearing what their kids were doing made me realize that I was expecting way too much from my girls." (Karen)

Bounce things off of your friends. When you are struggling in an area, get their insight regarding the situation. Another mom said she read books about parenting and children in order to keep a proper perspective.

Sharon suggests calling your children when you are away and listen to how small they sound on the phone. I am always amazed at how young my seven-year-old still sounds when I talk to her. It reminds me to treat her like a little girl, not a little adult.

longing for tomorrow

As moms it is easy to miss out on the joys of today because we are longing for tomorrow. I've heard moms say, "I can't wait till my daughter is potty trained" or "I will be so glad when my son starts kindergarten" or "I'll be a much better mom when my daughter is a little older." But each new stage will bring its own problems with it. Better to enjoy, and not miss, the moments of *today*.

One morning I (Laurie) was frantically trying to get to an early morning appointment with my two small children. Rushing around and struggling to get us all dressed, I was shouting orders at my little soldiers (ages three and six months). "Come on . . . hurry up, we gotta go!" (You know, preschoolers don't know what the word *hurry* means. You might as well say, "Come on, *slow down,* we're late." And it would have the same impact!) In the midst of my frenzied state that morning, Alec (the three-year-old) was trying to dress himself and couldn't quite figure out the snap on his pants. Looking up at me he asked the simple question, "Mommy, can you help me? I can't do it."

It wasn't a huge request, but that day it was "the straw that broke the camel's back." Bending to help him fix his pants, but irritated at having to do "one more thing," I snapped at him, "I can't wait till you are big enough to do this on your own!" Then suddenly, as if someone had lifted the shades in a dark room, the eyes of my mind were opened to the future. I heard a gentle voice say, "Laurie, someday he's not going to ask you for your help anymore. And you'll wish he would!"

From that day on I never again said, "I can't wait till . . ." My son is ten years old now, and he doesn't ask for my help very often. (I think the roles have changed. Now I have to ask him for help, especially with electronic things.) However, these days when he does ask for my help, I cherish every moment. I don't have to rush the days anymore; they rush by all on their own!

During those days, when I was in "survival mode," I remember sitting outside with my kids each afternoon waiting for my husband to come home from work. And like a cat pouncing on a ball of yarn I would meet him in the drive, ready to hand off the kids. I was ready for a break and some time to myself. I found myself constantly thinking about and longing for the weekend, summer vacation, or a night out with "the girls" to help me cope with the wearisome challenges of each day.

I found, however, that those "nights out" would come and go, and I would still be discontented with my mundane life the next day. Just being a mother didn't seem to have much significance, and I wasn't feeling very satisfied. What was my mission in life? Where was the fulfillment that I so longed for?

"I can't wait till this weekend," I heard myself telling a friend. "My husband and I are finally having a date." The only problem was that it was Monday—I had to make it through the whole week until the much-needed date would arrive. What would I do throughout the week? Would my children hear me wish for the weekend every time they spilled their juice, argued with each other, or came crying to tell me they were "hurt" again?

I suddenly realized that by longing for the weekend I was wishing weeks of my life away. Precious days were being simply survived in order to make it to the oasis . . . the weekend, when my husband would be home. As I felt God tugging at my heart, I had to ask for forgiveness for rushing the precious moments He had given me each day. It is so easy to wish for tomorrow and miss the little blessings of today.

My friend Janet helped me gain perspective one day when she told me about the impatience of her five-year-old son. They were vacationing in Colorado and had hiked up to a beautiful waterfall. All her children, along with their cousins, were having a wonderful time playing at the waterfall, when the five-year-old spotted a waterfall a little farther up the mountain. He ran to her and asked, "Mommy, can we go play up there . . . can we, please?" She told him, "Maybe in a little while. Go play." A few minutes passed and he came back to her with the same question. Again she encouraged him to "go play" and promised that they would go up to the other waterfall in a while. After the fourth time he approached her, begging, "Can we go up there now, Mom?" she pulled him aside and said, "Honey, because you are wanting to go up to the other waterfall so badly, you are missing all the fun right here." Then she said to me, "Laurie, don't miss the moments you are in *right now* by longing for what might be in the future."

What words of wisdom! As long as we are focusing on where we *wish we were* instead of being thankful in the midst of *where we are,* we will be discontented. Isn't it true that we can spend way too much energy either looking ahead at what is coming or focusing on our past? In either case we cannot enjoy *today*. Today is a gift. Make the most of it with those you love—don't miss it!

"These Days"

I've heard it said a hundred times, "Enjoy it while it lasts."
They say these days will come and go and then will be the past.
I know it's true they'll grow up soon; how can I make it last?
These days slip by so fast.
These days are here, these days are now.
Help us treasure every day somehow.
Don't look back or up ahead. Just live and love today.
These days are here and then they're gone;
Help us be content, they won't last long.
For we only have these days.
("These Days," words by Laurie Hilliard,
music by Sharon and Pat Autry and Laurie Hilliard, 1999,
from the album *Hold You, Mommy*)

From the wisdom of their perspective, the gray-haired angels taught me to "enjoy the moments," to notice and appreciate the simple things today that I'll cherish and miss tomorrow. Through them, God changed my perspective from "I have no life" to "It's a wonderful life, and I don't want to miss it!"

He can do the same thing for you! Embracing right where you are as a mom will bring peace and contentment to your days. When you allow God to show you that the role of "mom" is one of significance and value, you will find freedom, fulfillment, and purpose in life. Then you'll be on your way to becoming a "mom . . . and loving it!"

stop, drop, and restore your soul

Moving from pre-baby life to life with children is quite an adjustment for any woman. Many times we think, *All I'm doing is adding a kid to my life; what could be so hard about that? Everyone else does it . . . what's the big deal?* I found that the job of motherhood is more difficult than I'd ever planned on or could have imagined. It is a much more demanding and challenging job than I was prepared for.

As moms it is easy to become frustrated and resentful when we are unable to continue on with our "normal" life, with time for ourselves. Our lives are suddenly dictated by the eating/nap schedules and moods of our children and not our own desires or choices anymore. Guilt overwhelms us when we experience feelings of discontentment and resentment, and so we work harder and longer as we strive to be a "better mom."

When we as women embrace where God has placed us (in whatever stage of mothering it might be), we will begin to realize that contentment can be attained as we surrender to God's call right where we are. We will be able to view the interruptions, distractions, and challenges of the position as God's divine purpose for our lives. All of it together will result in our becoming a mom . . . who loves it!

1. What have you caught yourself saying that reflects your desire to rush *your* days or *your children's* days?
2. In what ways are you expecting your children to be "little adults"? List ways in which you may be "hurrying them" into adulthood.
3. What do you often dream about or long for that you believe will bring you happiness and contentment? What are you looking forward to right now that makes your days long and your temper short?
4. What are some things in your life that you may be taking for granted? What are you thankful for right where you are?

Father,

I want to be a happy, fulfilled woman, but I confess that many times I look for contentment outside of where I am. Help me embrace where You have me today, to accept it and find joy in the moment. Help me to see that my mission right now is caring for my children. Help me to change my perspective from seeing my kids as interruptions to seeing them as Your primary purpose for my life. Help me to be "okay" with where I am. Give me creativity and patience as I become the mom You want me to be. Lord, I can't make these changes on my own; I need You to change me. I surrender! In Jesus' name I pray. Amen.

making the most of the moments

When the four walls are closing in, or when you want to go hide from your kids instead of be with them, try these helpful suggestions:

1. **dear God** If you are struggling with feelings of frustration, discontentment, and resentment, write an honest letter to God (not holding back) about how you feel where you are. Share your struggles with a friend; you might be surprised to learn that they have experienced some of the same things!

2. **family photos** Get out a picture album (again) and look at it with your children. Tell them stories you remember about each situation.

3. **gray-haired angel alert!** The next time you meet a "gray-haired angel" tell her (or him), "Thank you for reminding me how precious the days are with my children."

4. **pray up as you pick up!** When picking up abandoned socks, toys, shoes, do what Jen does: Pray for your children while picking up their things instead of complaining about what you are doing. For example, "Lord, thank You for the little feet that go into these socks. May they walk according to Your ways. Thank You for the hands that play with these toys. May they do great things to glorify You!"

5. **thanks times ten** When you awaken each morning, ask God to help you see His purpose in your days, to see the moments with your children as divine appointments instead of interruptions. Make a list of ten things that you are thankful for right now, where you are. Hang it where you'll see it daily.

resources for moms

Anger
She's Gonna Blow, Julie Barnhill, Harvest House Publishers, 2001.
When Counting to Ten Isn't Enough, Kathy Collard Miller, Xulon Press, 2003.

Crisis Pregnancy/Post-Abortion Counseling
Focus on the Family, *www.family.org,* 800–395-HELP
www.mend.org

Embracing Parenthood
The Mission of Motherhood—Touching Your Child's Heart for Eternity, Sally Clarkson, WaterBrook Press, 2003.
The Power of a Positive Mom, Karol Ladd, Howard Publishing, 2001.
Real Moms: Exploding the Myths of Motherhood, Elisa Morgan and Carol Kuykendall, Zondervan, 2002.
Wired by God, Joe White, Tyndale House Publishing, 2004.
www.cherifuller.com.

Discipline
Creative Correction: Extraordinary Ideas for Everyday Discipline, Lisa Whelchel, Tyndale House Publishers, 2000.
The Five Love Languages of Children, Ross Campbell and Gary Chapman, Moody Press, 1997.

Grief
The Art of Helping: What to Say and Do When Someone Is Hurting, Lauren Littauer Briggs, Chariot Victor Publishing, 2003.
Empty Arms, Pam Vredevelt, Multnomah Publishers, Inc., 1984 (2nd ed. 1994).
An Empty Cradle, A Full Heart, Christine O'Keeffe Lafser, Loyola Press, 1998.

Grieving the Child I Never Knew, Kathe Wunnenberg, Zondervan, 2001.

I Can't Find a Heartbeat, Melissa Sexson Hanson, Review and Herald Publishing, 1999.

I'll Hold You in Heaven, Jack Hayford, Regal Books, 1990.

Letter to a Grieving Heart: Comfort and Hope for Those Who Hurt, Billy Sprague and John MacMurray, Harvest House Publishers, 2001.

Mommy, Please Don't Cry: There Are No Tears in Heaven, Linda De-Ymaz, Multnomah Gifts, 2003.

Safe in the Arms of God: Truth From Heaven About the Death of a Child, John MacArthur, Thomas Nelson Books, 2003.

Someone I Loved Died (Please Help Me, God), Christine H. Tangvald, Chariot Victor Publishing, 1988.

We Were Gonna Have a Baby, But We Had an Angel Instead, Pat Schwiebert (available at *www.griefwatch.com*).

When God Doesn't Make Sense, James C. Dobson, Tyndale House Publishers, 1993.

Marriage

The Love List—Eight Little Things That Make a Big Difference in Your Marriage, Drs. Les and Leslie Parrott, Zondervan, 2002.

The Seven Conflicts—Resolving the Most Common Disagreements in Marriage, Tim and Joy Downs, Moody Publishers, 2003.

Music

Hold You, Mommy, 2MOMS, 1999 (available at *www.momand lovingit.org*).

Mom Organizations

- Hearts at Home (*www.hearts-at-home.org*), 309–888-MOMS

  They seek to professionalize motherhood. After all, it is a full-time, more like all-the-time, job. They hold conventions in different parts of the country for moms.

- Heart of the Home (*www.heartofthehome.org*)

  This is an organization in California that holds a conference each year. Janet Ables, the founder, is available as a speaker. You can contact her at 661–861–5540.

- Moms in Touch International (*www.momsintouch.org*), 800-949-MOMS (6667)

  A prayer ministry with two or more moms who meet for one hour each week to pray for their children, their schools, their teachers, and school administrators. The four step format also works for preschool moms, homeschooling moms, moms of adult children, and grandmas.

- MOPS International (Mothers of Preschoolers) *www.mops.org*
  Specifically designed to meet needs of mothers with preschool children, this is a ministry available to moms almost everywhere in the country. Check their Web site for a group in your area. They usually meet twice a month. It's a great way to meet other moms.

Other Resources

To order Janie's book of poetry, *Walking in the Shadow of the Cross,* e-mail her at Janella@momandlovingit.org. The cost is $12.00. (Sharon and Laurie receive no compensation for the sale of Janie's book.)

FAQs about having a personal relationship with Jesus

1. *Should I tell anybody about asking Jesus into my heart?*

Think of accepting Christ as your second birthday. That's where "born again" comes from. "Therefore, if anyone is in Christ, he is a new creation; The old has gone, the new has come!" (2 Corinthians 5:17).

It's a celebration! You *were* headed for a life of despair and an eternity of no hope in hell. But *now* you have the promise of life with Jesus on the earth and in heaven. Your "forever" has been changed! Tell someone whom you know will encourage you, someone who can celebrate with you. Romans 10:10 (THE MESSAGE) says, "With your whole being you embrace God setting things right, and then you say it, right out loud: 'God has set everything right between him and me!'"

Telling somebody is not what saves you, but telling someone can help you start growing in your relationship with Christ. It is nothing to be ashamed of.

2. *Does this mean I'll never do anything wrong again? I know people who say they are Christians, but I've seen them sinning.*

You need to know that just because you've asked Jesus to come into your life, it doesn't mean that you'll never sin again. You're still human. Remember to be patient with yourself. Growing in Christ is a gradual process. Second Corinthians 3:18 (THE MESSAGE) explains: "Our lives [are] gradually becoming brighter and more beautiful as God enters our lives and we become like him."

But when you do sin, ask Him for forgiveness to keep your communication clear. *When we sin, it temporarily blocks the fellowship, but it doesn't break the relationship.* Here are some great verses about God's forgiveness:

> *If we confess our sins, he is faithful and just and will forgive us our sins and purify us from all unrighteousness.* (1 John 1:9)

> *For I will forgive their wickedness and will remember their sins no more.* (Hebrews 8:12)

> *As high as heaven is over the earth, so strong is his love to those who fear [respect] him. And as far as sunrise is from sunset, he has separated us from our sins. As parents feel for their children, GOD feels for those who fear him.* (Psalm 103:11–13 THE MESSAGE)

Just like we should ask a friend for forgiveness if we have offended them, the same is true with God. It's hard to talk to someone when there has been trouble between you.

3. *What do I do when I think maybe I'm not really a Christian?*

This is always a big question because invariably, after we accept Jesus, we will find ourselves doubting that our decision to follow Christ was genuine. I had doubts until a friend told me, "Before you're a Christian, Satan doesn't want you thinking about Jesus. But after you accept Him, all Satan can do is make you doubt your decision."

Something else that can bring doubts is when you have unconfessed sin. Again sin temporarily blocks the fellowship but doesn't break the relationship. Nothing can break the relationship. John 10:27–30 (THE MESSAGE) says: "My sheep recognize my voice. I know them, and they follow me. I give them real and eternal life. They are protected from the Destroyer for good. No one can steal them from out of my hand. The Father who put them under my care is so much greater than the Destroyer and Thief. No one could ever get them away from him. I and the Father are one heart and mind." And Romans 8:38–39 says: "For I am convinced that neither death nor life, neither angels nor demons, neither the present nor the future, nor any powers, neither height nor depth, nor anything else in all creation, will be able to separate us from the love of God that is in Christ Jesus our Lord."

It can be helpful to write down the date you asked Jesus into your heart, as well as how you felt and thoughts you had. Having that to look at when you're doubting can remind you that your decision to follow Christ was real.

4. *The Bible is a big book. Where should I start reading?*

I asked a pastor friend of mine (Mr. Bob), and he said to start at the beginning. He encouraged me to tell you that reading the Bible is like plowing a field. When you get to a rock in a field, you go around it but you keep plowing. In the Bible there will be some rocks (like the lists of who begat whom, and some confusing things). Go around those rocks, skip them, then keep going. God will open your heart and teach you so much from just reading His message to you.

5. *What version of the Bible do you recommend?*

Personally, we use the *New International Version* (NIV) and also *The Message*. *The Message* is written in plain language like we would talk to each other. Sometimes that is easier to understand.

Endnotes

chapter one

1. Elisa Morgan and Carol Kuykendall, *Real Moms: Exploding the Myths of Motherhood* (Grand Rapids, MI: Zondervan, 2002), 97.
2. Dan Allender, Ph.D., "Children Raise Us," *Parentlife*, April 2004, 26.

chapter three

1. Mimi Doe, *Busy But Balanced* (New York: St. Martin's Press, 2001). Quote taken from article by Karalee Miller, Star-Telegram.com, Aug. 24, 2004.
2. Kenneth Sanderfer, "The Single Parent Q and A," *Christian Single*, April 2004, 26.
3. Lindy Batdorf, "Chaos Theory," *Christian Parenting Today*, Spring 2004, 34.
4. Stephanie Nickel, "Clutter Control," *Christian Parenting Today*, Fall 2004, 9.
5. Internet source: "In His Service" Web site (*www.inhis.com*). Updated October 28, 2004.

chapter five

1. Julie Barnhill, *She's Gonna Blow* (Eugene, OR: Harvest House, 2001), 129.
2. Elisa Morgan and Carol Kuykendall, *Real Moms* (Grand Rapids, MI: Zondervan Publishing, 2002), 97.
3. Sally Clarkson, *The Mission of Motherhood* (Colorado Springs, CO: WaterBrook Press, 2003), 54.

chapter seven

1. Julie Barnhill, "Scandalous Grace," *Today's Christian Woman*, May/June 2004, 46.
2. Rick Warren, *The Purpose-Driven Life* (Grand Rapids, MI: Zondervan, 2002), 253.

chapter eight

1. Ted Baehr, *The Media-Wise Family* (Colorado Springs, CO: Chariot Victor Publishing, 1998), 82.

2. Amy Veits, "Give a Little Bit," *Christian Parenting Today*, Summer 2004, 42.

3. Ted Baehr, *The Media-Wise Family*, 77.

4. Taprina K. Milburn, "Innocent Gossip?" *www.family.org/pastor/pfmarried/a0016830.cfm, Focus on the Family* Magazine, Feb. 2000.

5. Jim Burns, "Media-Wise Parents," *Christian Parenting Today*, Fall 2004, 24.

6. Mary Farrar, *Choices* (Sisters, OR: Multnomah Publishers, 1994), 74, 76.

chapter eleven

1. Gary Chapman and Ross Campbell, *The Five Love Languages of Children* (Chicago, IL: Moody Publishing, 1997).

chapter twelve

1. Sally Clarkson, *The Mission of Motherhood* (Colorado Springs, CO: WaterBrook Press, 2003), 131.

2. *The Today Show*, Matt Lauer and Katie Couric, August 19, 2004.

chapter fourteen

1. Dr. James Dobson, *When God Doesn't Make Sense* (Carol Stream, IL: Tyndale House Publishers, 1993), 9.

2. Michele Howe, *Going It Alone* (Peabody, MA: Hendrickson Publishers, 1999), 4.

3. Larry Yeagley, *Grief Recovery* (Muskegon, MI: Self-published, 1981), 24.

Mom and Loving It Ministries presents more ways to become a Mom and LOVE It!

Hold You, Mommy consists of twelve songs written from a mother's perspective, encouraging moms to make the most of every moment with their children. The music on this CD can help transform a mom's life from simply surviving the day to really enjoying and treasuring the time she has with her kids.

Mom and Loving It Conferences

If you find yourself hiding in your closet for some alone time, or jogging an extra lap around the block before you face the family again, the time is right! You are due for some "time out," not just to do nothing but to *invest* in your role as mom. Visit our Web site to find a conference in your area or get information on how to bring Sharon and Laurie to your community. You'll laugh, cry, and go home ready to hug your children.

"The songs and the stories you shared help me remember I'm not alone in how I feel when the going gets tough. Your presentation reminded me to CELEBRATE this stage of life, because it will not last forever. Thank you for touching my heart. You've given me a gift that will last a lifetime." —Kristina, California

Mom-Inspired Resources

At the Mom and Loving it Web site you can learn more about the ministry, hear the music by Laurie and Sharon, sign up to receive their bi-monthly newsletter, and find other mom-inspired resources.

Sharon and Laurie would love to hear your thoughts about their book *Mom . . . and Loving It! Finding Contentment in Real Life.* Contact them at:

mail@momandlovingit.org

or

Mom and Loving It
P.O. Box 286
Whitesboro, TX 76273
888-95-2MOMS
www.momandlovingit.org